MY FIRST LOVE
TRUE LOVE BEGINS IN HIM

WRITTEN BY SONJA P. DRUMMOND

Newark, Delaware

My First Love
True Love Begins in Him
Copyright © 2009 Sonja P. Drummond

ISBN: 978-0-9823865-0-7

Published by:
Destiny & Purpose Publishing
P. O. Box 10963
Wilmington, DE 19850-0963
Orders: Destiny&PurposePublishing.com
http://Destiny&PurposePublishing.com

All rights reserved. No part of this book may be reproduced or transmitted in any form or by any means, electronic or mechanical, including photocopying, recording, or by any information storage and retrieval system, without written permission from the author, except for the inclusion of brief quotations in a review.

Scripture quotations marked AMP are from the Amplified Bible. Old Testament copyright © 1965, 1987 by the Zondervan Corporation. The Amplified New Testament copyright © 1954, 1958, 1987 by the Lockman Foundation. Used by permission.

Scripture quotations marked KJV are from the King James Version of the Bible.

Scripture quotations marked NIV are from the Holy Bible, New International Version. Copyright © 1973, 1978, 1984, International Bible Society. Used by permission.

Scripture quotations marked NKJV are from the New King James Version of the Bible. Copyright © 1979, 1980, 1982 by Thomas Nelson, Inc., publishers. Used by permission.

Unattributed quotations are by Sonja P. Drummond

Copyright Ó 2007

Library of Congress Cataloging-in-Publication Data

DEDICATION

This journey is dedicated, first and foremost, to:

My Lord, my God, my everything.

Lord, I thank You for choosing me and giving me purpose that I pray will be a life-changing experience for my family and those You have chosen to read this.

I thank you, Eric, for sharing this journey with me from the very beginning. If it had not been for you, I do not know if I would be writing these words now. You are everything a mother could ever hope for in a young man. You're God's man—a soldier, a warrior, an ambassador, an absolute powerhouse. Be a leader, never a follower, unless you're following God. And whatever you do, always remember these things first: pray, trust, and wait on God.

I call you "Mercy."

Asia, because of you God allowed me to see how the enemy tries to take us out even before we can speak and at many times before we enter this world. But you know most importantly He showed me that His power succumbs that of the enemy. I never knew happiness and the importance of protecting your own until I knew you. God has given you an awesome gift called joy. So many of us desire and long for it, but few of us tend to allow ourselves to enjoy it. Never allow anyone to steal your joy. You are God's virtuous woman—an encourager, a warrior, an ambassador, a woman after God's own heart. Use the wisdom God has given you to make earth-shaking breakthroughs to those who have mistaken the enemy from the Lord.

I call you "Joy."

Samara, I cannot describe in words all that you mean to me. All I can say is thank You, Jesus…thank You, Jesus…thank You, Jesus! Thank you for holding me accountable and not allowing me to hide my sins from the world. You are of a generation of powerful, unstoppable, unmovable, and victorious soldiers for Christ. No devil will ever be able to stop you because of the hedge of protection about you. Your name—Samara—means "guarded by God." You are a mighty soldier, a victorious woman, fully equipped with the ammunition of the Lord. Knowing you was coming to know God's forgiveness and complete love He has for me. I trust Him more now than I have ever, and my journey has just begun.

I call you "Deliverance."

Alexia, God has demonstrated to me through your existence that He is a God that fulfills His promises. I have always had a desire to have twins, and He has filled that desire in my heart through you and Alexandria. Hallelujah to my Father the Almighty! Hallelujah to my Savior, the Lord Jesus Christ! Hallelujah to the Gentleman, the Holy Spirit, who rules and reigns in my heart! Alexia, you are a mighty woman after God's own heart. You are joy unspeakable. You are determination insurmountable. You are the voice that will speak God's promises, His goodness, and His faithfulness.

I call you "God promises."

Alexandria, three pounds and fourteen ounces of power and strength! Your birth size reminds me of Deborah, the Israelite judge. You may not have been seen with physical strength or might, but you symbolize authority and power from our mighty God above.

Although you were born last by eight minutes, you are a leader and not a follower. You will be FIRST and not LAST. Eight means, "NEW BEGINNINGS." When I looked for a miracle from God during the time I carried you and your sister, God showed me, as I looked in the mirror at my large belly, "These are your miracle." It was at that moment that I truly surrendered in my heart my will for His. His will has fulfilled His promises and has answered prayers, and this is truly just the BEGINNING. You are a leader. You are a powerhouse. You are God's voice.

I call you, "God answers."

TABLE OF CONTENTS

DEDICATION iii
INTRODUCTION ix
CAST xiii

SCENE I 17
   Now Your Name Is Destiny
SCENE II 51
   Betrayed With a Kiss
SCENE III 103
   The Sting of a Bee
SCENE IV 121
   Walking in My Destiny

CLOSING 149
ABOUT THE AUTHOR 157
ORDER PAGE 163

INTRODUCTION

This is a story about my destiny—the life I tried to keep concealed that was not mine to begin with. God had a plan for me before He placed me in the womb of my mother. His plan was to use all that I was ashamed of and bring those things out in the open. He wanted me to reveal myself so that He may heal my wounds and make me whole.

I remember always wanting to help others I saw in pain, especially the women in my life, but I never knew how. I never understood with helping others, at times, comes a price. I would have to experience the things that those bleeding women were going through in order to enable me to understand their pain. I would have to deplete all my resources and be mocked and ridiculed by my family, friends, and community in order to get to the place of knowing that God would never forsake me.

I had to crawl through the crowds of people as the blood continued to flow, although the bleeding would not possess the power to bring forth death (God had His hands on me)—crawling, realizing that if I could just find the answer, find that one man who would love me, I would become whole.

Regardless of my failures, regardless of my flaws, the simple fact was that I was bleeding left with nothing, and no one wanted me, no one but Jesus. If I could just touch the hem of His garment, He would heal me.

This is the journey I had to go through so that others would not have to. I had to shed rivers of tears so that others may be filled with the joy of laughter.

You might ask, "Is the desire of wanting to help others worth it?" Can any person who went through so much love God and not be angry with Him? Yes, they can. Because you see, if I had not experienced those things, I would never come to know the love of God. I would have never come to know the true meaning of love. I would have never gotten to know Him personally for myself. I would have never come to know that He is LOVE.

God represents true love. This love is unadulterated, unconditional, unchangeable, and unending. His love cancels out every evil deed, every form of abuse, every tear, and every bruise that I ever received and experienced.

When you go through life without God, you find yourself defining your life by what the world and people say it is or should be. You will seek answers you have been searching for in people, and when they fail you, never satisfying your need and never answering your questions, you become lost. How could you not when you rely on answers from others who are lost as well?

When you look in the mirror you don't comprehend what you see; most likely you don't like that person staring back at you. All you have are preconceived notions and false assumptions of who you believe you are. This is based on your experiences and spoken words that go against every good thing God says about you. This was how I was conditioned to believe for years.

I was lost, believing in others who were lost as well, until I began to seek answers from God. Who better to ask than the Creator Himself? He was there the entire time, waiting for me to call on Him, waiting for me to let Him in. Once I did, the scales began to fall off my eyes, and the wall I had built up to protect my wounded heart, God began to tear down. This was so that He could fully heal my heart without leaving a scar. I thank God for all that I have gone through and for His grace. If it had not been for His grace, I would still be wondering, "Why?"

I believe our lives are like plays being lived. You are the main character of your play, and God is the narrator, writer, producer, and director. He will show you the end, but He decides what parts of the middle to reveal to you. He will not show you everything because you may not want to get to the end. Allow Him to take you through and refine you so that you will come out as pure gold. He doesn't want to do anything that hurts you, and He will never leave you alone. Go through life with Him so that you may live a life of victory and abundance. He will take you to the light at the end of the tunnel. Without Him you will only come to a dead end, and along the way you'll continue to live in cycles of torment emotionally, spiritually, and, for many, physically. You can't make it in this world on your own because at the end you will be all alone, without hope, with shattered dreams, and with an unfulfilled purpose. When I leave this world I may not know and understand everything that has happened to me, but one thing is for certain: I will leave knowing and experiencing just how good God is.

I must say that the purpose of this book is to deliver you so that you may discover God personally in order for you to walk in your destiny and the purpose God has for you. The purpose of sharing my life with you is not so you would know all the ugly things I did or the things that have been done to me.

This is not any ordinary autobiography just for the purpose of telling "my story." I am sharing with you so that you may see what God has done for me. And if He did it for me, He will do it for you.

Finally, the purpose of this book is not to offend or hurt anyone. I have changed names in order to protect the identity of those I speak of. It begins in Scene I where I started to search and find my true identity—an identity not based on the opinions of others, false mind-sets, or the past, but on God who is the past, present, and future. What better place to begin this journey?

A Journey From Abuse to a Victorious Life!

My eyes made their way back to his. They were fierce as fire, like a lion ready to attack his enemy trying to invade his territory. Yanna brought his hand down and back-slapped me. Immediately, I felt a sting so painful my whole right side felt numb. I could see stars floating in mid-air like a cloud of fairy tale dust. My ears began ringing and throbbing. I wasn't sure if my teeth were still intact, or whether my eyes would swell up like an injured boxer on his tenth round.

The pain was more than I could imagine, but Yanna continued to ask the question, "Do you believe him?" My stubbornness would not allow any answer except "Yes." But the question was no longer a question but more of a cadence call. When I ask you, "Do you believe him?" you say "No." Being the strong-willed person that I am, I refused to give in. With the last blow to my face, I could no longer keep my balance. I felt a warm ooze seep from my nostrils as my balance gave out. Gravity won, it was stronger than my will.

At twelve I witnessed my mother being physically abused, and at seventeen I was physically abused. Join me as I share with you my path from substance abuse to freedom from substances, from a victim of domestic violence to victor over my abuse, and from searching for love in all the wrong places to finding the Love I searched for my entire life...my First Love.

CAST

Name	Meaning
Lorna	Lost, forlorn, forsaken
Angel	Messenger
Jerah	Mercy of God
Alisa	Joy
Hannah	Grace, gracious, merciful
Yanna	To oppress, maltreat
Amira	To say, tell, name, promise
Amita	Friend, colleague, companion
Theresa	Bold, courageous
Emma	Mother
Maoz	Strength, courage
Achisamach (Ach)	My brother is my support: Ach—brother Samach—my support
Ezriella	God is my support
Chana	Compassionate, gracious
Magen	Shield, protector, defender

Name	Meaning
Davona	Gift
Jonathon	God has given
Tobias	God is good, goodness of God
Bryanna	One who is nobly born and eloquent
Yovar	To lament, cry
Koby	Nickname for Jacob meaning supplant, grip by heel
Jacob	Supplant, deceive; grip by the heel
Gideon	Brave soldier
Edward	Happy guardian
Bernadette	Bold as a bear
Khara	Beloved or beautiful face
Yedidah (Didi)	Friend or beloved; Didi (short form of Yedidah)
Tamir	Tall, stately, like the palm tree
Ufara	To lead, leader
Zephi	Overseer, guardian, spectator
David	Beloved
John	God is gracious
Maxine	Great

Scene I begins with a young lady named Lorna. Lorna did not know who she was, which resulted in her not knowing her purpose in life. In her despair she thought the only way out was to give up; however, a visitation would give her some hope that her purpose for being was for something far greater than she could ever imagine. About seventeen years later Lorna would begin writing in her journal about her experiences in her walk with God.

The scene starts with Lorna at ten years old. She never really felt loved, nor did she love herself. Her mother, a single parent, worked long hours to provide Lorna with all she believed her daughter needed. But what Lorna really needed was love.

Lorna lay on her couch after consuming half a bottle of aspirin because she wanted the pain to end. Lorna was speaking to herself, but she never knew someone was always listening. Lorna went to church every Sunday by herself because she knew it would make her mother happy, but she also found joy in attending. She would do anything to make her mother happy, but nothing she did ever seemed good enough.

Lorna knew about God, but she never knew who He was and that He was listening to her cries. Why should she? He never seemed to answer back until this day when she receives an unexpected visitation from one of His messengers.

Scene I

Now Your Name Is Destiny

But you are a chosen generation, a royal priesthood, a holy nation, His own special people, that you may proclaim the praises of Him who called you out of darkness into His marvelous light; who once were not a people but are now the people of God, who had not obtained mercy but now have obtained mercy.
(1 Peter 2:9-10, NKJV)

Lorna: I feel so alone. Why doesn't anybody love me?

The Angel (with a sweet alluring voice): Hello Lorna.

Lorna: Who are you? (Stuttering) W-w-where did you come from?

The Angel: Do not be afraid, Lorna. I am a messenger sent from God.

Lorna: Why would God send you here?

The Angel: Because He loves you. He knows you are hurting, and He is hurting too.

Lorna (starting to cry): Why would God love me? No one does. I am always left alone. Nobody understands.

The Angel: You are His child. (Lifting Lorna's head by her chin) And He is always with you. God understands you more than you understand yourself.

Lorna: Then why would God allow me to be in so much pain? Why does He let people hurt me?

The Angel: Pain and sorrow do not come from God, but He will use it for your good. Everything that happens is for a reason. He wants you to know the love you long for is in Him. You will never be able to get this love from anyone. Not a man, not your mother...Lorna, not even your father. For God is love.

Lorna (in frustration): I don't understand God's love. If I can't see Him or feel Him....N-n-no. If God loves me, then tell Him to take me away from here! There's too much pain in my life. I don't want to live anymore!

The Angel: You don't have to see or touch a person to know the love they have for you. True love is greater than anything physical, and God's love for you is greater than that. His love lasts a lifetime, not just a mere moment. Your senses could never grasp the sweetness of His love. Lorna, God has a plan for you, so you have to stay here a little while longer. (Turning away) I must go now. (Pauses, looks back) He wants me to tell you one more thing. You will no longer be called Lorna. Now He will call you "Destiny."

Selections from Lorna's journal, the beginning of her journey from being lost to discovering her destiny...

May 31, 2000
It's been nineteen days since I've signed the Knight in Shining Armor contract agreeing that I would let God reconstruct me in order to be prepared for the mate He had intended for me to be with. This man will fear God and will have a wonderful relationship with Him.

I am very determined to live the way the Lord wants me to. I have got to stop the continual cycle of unhealthy relationships that have begun as far back as my grandfather (and maybe even further back). I have to, number one, have God be the man in this family and, number two, teach my children to walk the pathway of God. I love my children, and I am responsible for them. I realize that Alisa and Jerah are God's children, and I have to respect them and love them and teach them to be strong in Christ. I must teach them how to love themselves, love God, and love others.

I have been wondering what my purpose is (besides raising my children). I am waiting for the Lord to let me know. I have so many ideas, but I'm not sure, and I know that when the Holy Spirit tells me my purpose, I will be 100 percent sure, and right now I am not. Also, when the right person finds me, I will be certain. But I'm so afraid of how long it will take. I understand that the Lord must get me ready first, and that is what scares me. I just pray that He will give me strength to get through that period and that in the meantime He will reveal to me my other purpose besides raising my children. Thank You, Lord.

July 22, 2000
"God, anoint me with a new spirit..."

Why was it so difficult for those words to come forth from my mouth? I thought I might forget the series of words that I was told to repeat. No, not these words; they were only but a few. This brother and sister in Christ (a married couple that God had chosen for a great purpose) were there praying for me. We held hands as we stood in a circle of an enormous home that God had blessed them with. They were waiting on me to repeat the words: "God, anoint me with a new spirit."

I will give you a new heart and put a new spirit in you; I will remove from you your heart of stone and give you a heart of flesh....Then you will remember your evil ways and wicked deeds, and you will loathe yourselves for your sins and detestable practices.

(Ezekiel 36:26, 31, NIV)

Why couldn't I say these seven words? Our words have so much power. I could even feel the power that these words possessed. Did I even want this power?

To whom much is given, much is required.

October 13, 2000
Well, my six months contract is almost up! My life has drastically changed, and all I would say is...whew!... Thank You, Father. Thank You for being my everything. Thank You for forgiving me, supporting me, not letting me down, or judging, condemning, or giving up on me. Thank You for loving me unconditionally! This is true love, something I have never felt before. It is genuine.

I finally comprehend what peace feels like. Thank You for giving me Your peace. Thank You for joy, hope, faith, and love. I am so blessed for having the opportunity to have two beautiful children who are healthy, intelligent, talented, and full of love and compassion. My mother, despite her pain, continues to love me and reach out to me. I pray that You open my father's eyes.

I understand that I no longer have to search for love, joy, or peace. They are all within me because of You. Thank You for the opportunity of having others strengthen me through their ministries. I hope to one day strengthen others through my ministry.

I know that certain things are going to happen for my family and myself at the right time, Your time. Continue to strengthen me, encourage me, and increase my faith. Let the love of God continue to dwell in my life, our life.

October 24, 2000
For the past couple of days I have felt great torment, so I have searched for the One who would release me from this bondage. He

has loved me, forgiven me, accepted me, and forgotten my sins. He knows that I am not perfect (this I see every day). He knows that I give my heart to Him even if I may stumble and try to give my heart to another one. No one could give me what He will give me.

Your grace and mercy, Your unconditional love, I long for. I submit my mind and heart to You, for the heart can be very deceiving, for lies are fed into the mind. When I felt ashamed, I still looked unto You. When I felt lost, I still looked unto You. When I felt joy, I still looked unto You. When I felt doubt, I still looked unto You. When I felt Your light, I still looked unto You. Father, I never stopped looking unto You. Thank You for Your mercy, Your grace, Your unconditional love.

November 10, 2000
For a moment of pleasure I disappointed You, Father. Please forgive me. I know that You have already forgiven me, but how can I forgive myself?

Help me, Lord, for I have done something out of Your will. All I wanted to do is please You. My heart was lonely, and I did not put my trust in You. I wanted love, to feel loved and cared for, which already came from You. From my sin I lost love, knowing the consequences that would come. I lost love for myself. I felt I lost the progress I had made because I lacked faith in You.

He doesn't love me or care for me in the way that I need and want. I let him use me. I used myself to fulfill a moment of carnal pleasure, and now I am left with spiritual pain. When will I grow? How will I know, Lord, that I have obtained the strength to resist this temptation? Why am I back where I have begun? My spirit, my soul, and my heart cry from the pain that the moment of pleasure can never replace.

I am sorry I disappointed You. I am sorry I disappointed myself. I am too much flesh and not enough spirit. Dear Father, fill me with Your joy again, even though I am ashamed to even ask for it. I miss it.

Increase in my life faith, trust, hope, patience, meekness, and the spirit of joy. These are all things I lost in that moment, the moment I believed that You bent Your head down and shook it back and forth in disappointment for my actions. But You already knew that I would sin against You.

That moment was not even worth a grain of sand of the joy You have brought in my life. Help me, Father, to know that it is still mine and that it is still here within me. For Your Son sacrificed His life so that I may have life. I am unworthy of the remissions of my sins given through His shed blood, but nonetheless I have received it. And I, of little faith, trust, and hope, forgot it all during that short moment of pleasure. Thank You for Your unconditional love.

Amen.

December 17, 2000
Today was an awesome day. This whole week was a blessing. Baking was a joy with Jerah. Lord, just continue to work on my patience and understanding with him. God, You really put in my heart that I expect too much from Jerah. Please lead me to what is right.

I pray that You are touching the hearts of Yovar, Lee, and their families, as well as my family. I pray that You are revealing to them what is in their hearts and are renewing their minds. Please continue to work on Yovar's mind; bless him, Lord, and protect him, please. Thank You.

Continue to change my heart, and continue to renew my mind as well. My heart believes that You are bringing me to enjoy our relationship before You bring my mate. Thank You.

Just please continue to strengthen me, encourage me, strengthen my trust in You, and have my faith grow stronger. I love singing for You and praising Your name. The next thing is piano lessons for all of us, and sewing for me. Continue to work through me so that I may be a blessing to all. I love You and thank You for coming into my life. Thank You for being a part of my children's lives and for protecting them and for saving all of us.

December 18, 2000
I am grateful for all You have done for my family and all that You will do. I have so many tests going on right now, but they cannot keep me from focusing on You. They are actually causing me to rely on You more.

I just cannot begin to thank You enough for all You have done for me, how You have renewed me and changed my heart. Please continue to strengthen my faith and my trust in You, to encourage me and strengthen me. Keep my eyes focused on You and not on my circumstances. Everything shall come to past.

December 23, 2000
Today was another blessed day. I can't even begin to imagine all the wonderful things, people, and experiences that the Lord is going to bless my children and me with despite all He has already done! I do imagine myself blessing people with the gifts the Lord has blessed me with—encouragement, cooking, and singing.

I want to learn dancing and piano playing and, of course, voice lessons. I want to be a tremendous blessing as a wife to a great loving, caring, understanding, humble, and faithful husband. Please don't leave out a trusting, loyal, encouraging, and patient friend to me and my kids.

After speaking with Pastor Melvin today, I started thinking of us in a manner of being more than just friends. So please help me there. I don't understand why I would be so intimidated by him. Lord, he's just a man who happens to be a pastor.

I just wondered if he would feel if I was good enough for him. Lord, please search my heart and lead me. Have Your way, and please, whatever Your will is, God, please have us remain good friends. Help us to build a strong Christian friendship. I don't know what he wants from me. I'm sure there's more beautiful women who have their lives together. Am I enough for him? Well, I know I'm good enough in Your eyes, but will I be in his eyes? Anyways—strong friendship at least. But if it's in Your will for something more, please let it be! Thank You! I love You.

January 20, 2001
I get so lonely, yet I feel in my heart that I must be silent and patient—the two things I struggle with. But You are my strength, and through You all things are possible. Without You I am nothing.

I have a vision that I will be blessed with all the things that I dreamed of and that I have asked for, in Your name. In my heart I know that it is already done. Praise God! Thank You for all of Your blessings!

I am truly blessed. My children and I are in good health and strength, but most importantly, we are saved. Thank You.

Help me and strengthen my faith. Remove doubt, worry, and fear from my life and replace it with joy, faith, strength, confidence, self-control, and a vision for my calling. I want to be a woman of great faith, joyful, and busy fulfilling my purpose in life. Search me, reveal me, and lead me. Amen.

Resurrection Day 2001
I praise Your name and give You thanks for being an awesome God! This is the very first Resurrection Day that I truly honored You and understood this day's purpose, to praise Your name, thank You, and love You.

My heart feels burdened. I do not want Yovar (or anyone) to hurt Alisa again. He almost took her life once, and I don't want him to get another chance to do that again. I know, God, that You have control. I know the entire situation is in Your hands and that You are going to bless it. Praise Your holy name.

What is my purpose? What am I called to do? I know at the right time it will be revealed that You will work it all out.

Thank You. It has been done.

January 14, 2003

There was something I learned through this journey of kingdom building—the power of the tongue.

Death and life are in the power of the tongue, and they who indulge in it shall eat the fruit of it [for death or life].
                                                    (Proverbs 18:21, AMP)

I never realized how our words could bring either death or life into our situations. My words used to be destructive and very foolish. I spoke profanity and cursed many people. If someone hurt me, I wished bad things would happen to them. I didn't realize what I was doing.

I was terribly abused in different ways, but I didn't understand how to deal with the pain in a healthy way. Once I began to know and understand God and His ways, I slowly discovered my ways were not like His, and I wanted to change.

> *For my thoughts are not your thoughts, neither are your ways my ways, declares the Lord.*
> (Isaiah 55:8, NIV)

The first step that would lead to change would be to ask God for His forgiveness. Second, I had to receive His forgiveness by believing it was mine.

> *But what does it say? "The word is near you; it is in your mouth and in your heart," that is, the word of faith we are proclaiming: That if you confess with your mouth, "Jesus is Lord," and believeth in your heart that God raised him from the dead, you will be saved. For it is with your heart that you believe and are justified, and it is with your mouth that you confess and are saved.*
> (Romans 10:8-10, NIV)

Belief could be a very difficult thing when you have been betrayed all your life. You have to get your mind thinking correct thoughts. And although things do not look favorable at the time does not mean they will not get any better. I had to start believing for better things not only in my life but also in the lives of my family. In the midst of doing that I needed to know who I was in Christ Jesus.

> *Therefore if anyone is in Christ, he is a new creation; the old has gone, the new has come!*
> (2 Corinthians 5:17, NIV)

Believe it and receive it. A part of me receiving and believing was to confess it out of my mouth. These are some of the things that I confessed.

July 1, 2001

Confessions

Regarding Jerah:

I confess with my mouth that my Father God has wonderful plans for my son. That the work You have started in Jerah, You will finish.

I believe, Father, that You have chosen Jerah to minister to millions of people in some way, to share the Word so that millions will give their lives to You.

I confess that Jerah will be more responsible for his belongings as well as others'. Jerah will make As and Bs this year in school, not Ds and Fs.

Jerah will stop lying and being disobedient to me and to You. Jerah will respect his teachers and other classmates.

I confess that Jerah will receive Your knowledge and wisdom and speak words of life, knowledge, and wisdom, not death to himself or others.

Jerah is a good person, and he will believe in himself. He will know who He is in Christ.

Regarding Alisa:

I confess with my mouth that Alisa will be a Proverbs 31 woman, a woman more precious than rubies or pearls. Alisa will use her strong willpower to lead people to You, Father, to share Your Word with them.

Alisa will have a successful, significant life and not fall into premarital sex or any type of fornication or sin due to the spirit of lust.

Alisa will not allow the spirit of greed or pride to keep her from following You. Alisa will be obedient to You and me.

Alisa will accept her father's and my past and forgive and love us both. Alisa will be a Godly woman, wife, and mother. Alisa will raise her children to be grounded in You.

Regarding my mate:

I confess with my mouth, God, that You have already chosen my mate and are preparing the both of us. Our main focus will be to love, obey, and follow You, Father.

My mate will respect You and all You have created. He will want to love and respect me. He will fear hurting You and me. He will want to take all the hard things out of my life, protect me, and want to give me more than I have ever wanted in life and work very hard to do so.

He will not look at other women with eyes of lust or hate. He will love me all of his days no matter how I look or what I do. My mate will respect my feelings and pray about discernment when we disagree about something.

He will help me raise our children (all of them) according to Your perfect will. He will not abuse me or our children in any way.

He will spend money wisely and invest wisely. He will not feel ashamed to get down on his knees and pray and ask for forgiveness. He will always want me to be safe.

My mate will be loyal to his friends, pastor, parents, me, and our children. He will be accountable to his pastor, people in authority, and his friends.

He will always take care of me and our children and himself physically, mentally, and, most of all, spiritually.

February 4, 2002
It has been a very long time since I have entered anything in this journal, and for some reason I think I'd better start over on a daily basis.

Well today, like any other day, I was stressed. Stressed about working for a boss that seemed to be so unfair when all along I was just ungrateful and dealing with the spirit of pride. Stressed about Jerah. He poured his heart out to me and I couldn't even respond. God, I don't know how to respond now. I don't know what to say to him. Is he right? Am I that terrible? Or is he using it as another excuse for not wanting to take responsibility for his actions? Or am I, on the hand other hand, not wanting to take responsibility for my part in this?

I feel that maybe I am the one messed up. Maybe I am not a good mother; maybe he needs someone better. NO! That's a lie. Then what am

I doing, God? Why am I so angry? The last time I felt joy for Jerah was when I saw him in Annie. He was wonderful, and I believed for the first time he knew it too. He reminded me of Maoz when he was in that musical as a bad wolf. Maoz was awesome! Totally talented and full of life.

All I know is that I love Jerah and know You brought us together for some reason. Why am I always so angry at him? Am I afraid of losing him the same way I lost Maoz?

So much talent, so much potential, and so much life, but always feeling like he had to be the center of attention. He thrived on people. If he was alone he would die, having to face the fact that he was hurting and didn't know how to show it, so he tried to cover it up with laughter, other people's laughter while he wept inside. Is this Jerah too? Am I the cause of his pain? If so, then why am I here? Why are we together, hurting one another?

January 14, 2003
This would be my third attempt at writing my autobiography. When I was 15 (a little time after I had Jerah), I just started writing the experience I had with getting pregnant at a very early age. For some reason, after the tenth page I stopped. I did not know why. I thought I wasn't a good enough writer, nor was I certain as to why I was even writing it. Well, I ended up tearing it all up into tiny pieces.

At that time I was staying with Jerah's babysitter's daughter's family. Chana, Magen, Davona, and Jonathan were an awesome family. I had never felt the family love like I did when I lived with them. I loved it there, and so did Jerah. I thought I had been placed in my new permanent home.

Chana came into my room with sheets of paper in her hand. It was the pages I had written taped back together. She told me she had read it and that I should finish it. But for some reason I just couldn't; therefore I didn't go any further. I am not sure what happened to those pages. After several years, I tried again, but was still unable to finish it. I would suddenly forget certain parts of my life or felt I just wasn't good enough to write. At least that is what I thought, but I had been deceived.

Although I stopped writing, the story remained in my heart. I wanted to share it, but I was a little afraid. Afraid of not being a good writer. Afraid of hurting the people that were involved in my life. But most of all I was afraid of being judged and condemned for the things I had done. I felt I should just keep it between God and me.

One day I discovered the reason why I could never complete the writing. I was ashamed and had not forgiven myself for the things I had done. I wanted to keep my life concealed, but this was Satan's attempt to abort my ministry.

That night into the morning of July 22, 2000, I realized that I had to write. I was uncertain of who it would be for, but my heart kept telling me, "Many."

But he who did not know and did things worthy of a beating shall be beaten with few [lashes]. For everyone to whom much is given, of him shall much be required; and of him to whom men entrust much, they will require and demand all the more.
(Luke 12:48, AMP)

Therefore judge nothing before the appointed time; wait till the Lord comes. He will bring to light what is hidden in darkness and will expose the motives of men's heart. At that time each will receive his praise from God.
(1 Corinthians 4:5, NIV)

I kept waiting for a clear answer and received it at an appointed time. Two vessels that submitted themselves before God several years ago were being used by God to give me His word. His presence was there all around us. His angels soaring through the air protecting me. For God had a plan for me, and He was revealing it to me the way He had thirteen years ago.

I wasn't sure if what I was trying to accomplish for over ten years was something God wanted, I wanted, or the Prince of Darkness wanted. I didn't understand why it was so difficult to write when I could easily, at any given time, write a ten-page letter without ceasing.

The darkness was exposed. It was so dark in this place that I had it tucked away. Each time I tried to complete writing this, I would tuck it deeper and deeper within the depths of my soul and my heart. But the spirit was no longer going to allow it to fester. He was not going to allow it to rot this temple of God any longer.

It was just rotting away the beauty within me, the beauty I knew was there but could not feel. My Father has transformed so much of me that others saw it, others felt it, but the one who did not see or feel it was the one it resided in. For she had a rotten, moldy, decaying part that needed to be cut away!

> *You are my lamp, O Lord; the Lord turns my darkness into light.*
>
> (2 Samuel 22:29, NIV)

As powerful as this darkness was within me, God's light was so much more powerful. He destroyed the darkness and allowed me to witness the fullness of His beauty, to feel the beauty of being the daughter He loves so much.

Today I woke up with a new spirit. This spirit was no longer filled with darkness. The light has revealed the heart of man, and in this case the (wo)man was me.

My heart was full of unforgiveness. Not of my mother who called me a whore one too many times, for she was dealing with the rottenness of unforgiveness herself. Or my father who was never truly a father to me, for he may not have had his father's and/or mother's protection and love that he needed. Nor was it the unforgiveness of friends, past relationships, or enemies.

> *For our struggle is not against flesh and blood, but against the rulers, against the authorities, against the powers of this dark world and against the spiritual forces of evil in the heavenly realms.*
>
> (Ephesians 6:12, NIV)

No, this unforgiveness was greater than any words or any act any person could do to you. I lived with this person all my life who I was unable to forgive. How could I? How could this person now stand before God as a new creature for all she had done? I was tired of thinking about all the ugly things she had done or the words she had said.

They were a disgrace to God. So each time the memories started to get life again from the mere act of thinking and meditating on them, she would tuck them away deep down inside of her.

This unforgiveness kept her in bondage for over ten years. How could I tell this person that I forgive her? How could I look her in the face? How could I...forgive myself? I knew all that I had done, all that I had said, the things that I thought only God and I needed to know. As I was tucking the memories of the acts, the thoughts, and words full of lust, full of hate, full of death deep inside, I was dying more and more each time.

Jesus...said, "With man this is impossible, but with God all things are possible."
(Matthew 19:26, NIV)

So as I stood in front of the mirror and gazed at the reflection staring back at me, and for the first time, the words came from my lips, "I forgive you."

Who can discern his errors? Forgive my hidden faults.
(Psalm 19:12, NIV)

Bear with each other and forgive whatever grievances you may have against one another. Forgive as the Lord forgave you.
(Colossians 3:13, NIV)

July 20, 2001
I could remember her now as if it were just yesterday. Lying on that burgundy couch with her chin resting on the end while her left arm dangled off the edge, her hand sweeping the carpet. She had large brown eyes that strangers thought were filled with life. But if you looked closer, you could see emptiness. She wanted to be loved. She wanted to feel as if she had a purpose for living.

"Why was I ever born, God?" She kept asking out loud as if someone were there to listen. But there was no one there as it had always been. She was alone. Questioning her existence was a repeated question in which she still received no answer. She chewed on the last orange-flavored children's aspirin that remained from the half full bottle she consumed just minutes ago. She would have taken something stronger but she always gagged when she tried to swallow pills. Who was she kidding? She couldn't even overdose right! The only thing that seemed to be on her side was that they were chewable.

"Did I do something bad in a previous life that You are punishing me for?" She believed she had been reincarnated only to endure the pain that she felt she caused to others in her past life. "I don't want to live anymore, please take me away from here."

Why couldn't she just be happy? At least she had a home, a nice big yard, and a dog she loved who would always listen and seemed to understand her tears. He would always lower his pointy ears while sitting on the top of his dog house listening to her cries or laughter, the latter she rarely experienced.

July 24, 2001 (The memories of when I was fifteen years old)
For the second time, I found myself desperately waiting. This time it was on the results of a pregnancy test. My thoughts rushed back to five years ago when I was lying on the couch after swallowing a bottle of pills, hoping death would come so the pain would end.

I continue to wait this time for an answer that, if unfavorable, could possibly end my life. However, if the response ended in my favor, I would be able to go about my now happy life, a life that took many years to get this way.

I was still lonely from time to time whenever my boyfriend wasn't around. If it were up to me, I'd have him around 24/7, but sneaking him around while my mom was home was definitely impossible. So I'd just invite him over when my mom was at work. I totally gave myself to him.

I know I was too young, but doesn't every fifteen-year-old girl in those days give it up to the one that they loved, especially if they loved you back? At least that was what I thought. Besides, my friend was twelve years old when her mom got her birth control pills and the guy she was sleeping with was around sixteen years old.

Oh, God, I almost forgot one of our classmates. I knew she was having sex. Everyone knew she was, with her big pregnant stomach. She was only fifteen! I was fifteen as well. Didn't she know about the withdrawal method, foam, etc.?

Scene I: Now Name Your Destiny

Alright, maybe Maoz and I didn't use protection all the time, but he would always withdraw. I was certain of that because I would see it. It looked really nasty, like egg white mixed with thick crushed aspirin.

I would just be happy to be alive. If I received bad news, my mom would know what I had been doing and kill me anyways. What am I trippin' about anyway? I don't belong here. Maoz loves me, and I know he wouldn't mess my life up like that. As I sit in this hard wooden chair waiting as my pee cooks in this weird microwave oven, my friend Amita peeked her head around the corner of the waiting area. She had her two fingers crossed. That will help. I'll cross my fingers also.

Amita and her little beady eyes and that walnut brown hair. Her hair was so curly and frizzy, resembling what could possibly be a nest turned upside down. I would even call her nest head. She didn't mind it though; she was really cool.

She and I had a lot in common. We were both being raised by our single moms and had no brothers or sisters living with us. We both lived in the same neighborhood, in nice houses with nice big yards, and we both had pets. But she had a cat and I had a dog. Oh yeah, and her mom was an alcoholic and my mom wasn't. My mom couldn't drink a sip of alcohol without being knocked out the rest of the night. Sometimes I wish she had, maybe she would have been much nicer.

My mom wasn't that bad, she just called me names, sometimes. She would call me stupid, hardheaded, lazy, and black nigger or lazy black American nigger. I could deal with the other names, although they still hurt, but I could never stand the black nigger comments. She would always talk about my dad and his family. She'd tell me how lazy they were, how they were all on welfare, and how all the girls got pregnant at a young age. I hated it every time! It wasn't fair! They were never around to defend themselves, especially my dad. But it was his fault anyway that I was stuck with her all by myself. Why did he have to go out to clubs all the time and drink and smoke dope? Why did he have to be with other women? If my dad was here for me he could defend me, but he wasn't because he couldn't be the dad or husband he was supposed to be. All he did was run away.

If you didn't like niggers, then why did you marry one? Huh? Why did you have a baby by one, huh? I never said that to her though, nor did I tell her that I wished she was black.

I knew that if I had a black mom she would understand me. She would have spent more time with me. She wouldn't leave me alone 6:30 in the morning until 4:00 in the afternoon. I needed you around! I needed you to talk to and to understand how I felt, how lonely I was! But that's all right because I have Maoz. He'll never leave me or call me names. He loves me. I know because he shows me every day when you're not around.

Now my butt was starting to get numb. It seemed as if the dial on the microwave had not moved in hours. I looked up at this weird poster of a human hand holding a baby's foot. What was so weird about this poster was that the foot was so small it fit in between the person's two fingers. I squinted my eyes to read the fine print below the foot…"This is the foot of a 10 week old baby." Wow! That was deep! That baby must have been a dead baby from an abortion or something. No way a baby that little could live; even I knew that.

The lady got up and walked to the microwave oven and got the cup of pee that I had brought just an hour ago from home. I can't believe I rode my bike clear across town holding a brown bag with a cup of my morning pee. It had to be "the first urine sample of the morning," the lady on the other end of the telephone said as I was getting all the information I needed to make this appointment. That'll be easy, I thought, since I'd been peeing a million times every morning for the past couple of days, or maybe weeks, who knows, who cares? It really doesn't matter.

I looked at the doorway again to see if Amita would be looking. She wasn't. I crossed my fingers extra tight until it seemed as if the blood stopped flowing, and I knew that Amita was doing the same.

"Well," the lady said, "it's positive." Positive? I thought to myself.

Positive that I'm not or positive that I am? "Positive?" I repeated after her dumbfounded, because I did feel dumb since I really didn't know what she meant. I was waiting for a yes/no answer, not a positive answer. I don't talk like that! "The test results came up positive. You are pregnant," she said, answering my yes/no question.

I just stared at the cup of pee hoping I didn't hear what I just did, knowing that the test results had to be wrong.

"What are you going to do?" she asked.

"I don't know," I replied. "Is there any way it could be wrong? Is there any other test I could take?" I was not going to give up. I knew this had to be a joke. This couldn't be happening to me! "Well, the results are 98.9% accurate, but you could get a blood test that is much more accurate than this test."

July 25, 2001
I can't even remember what words were said while Amita and I rode our bikes back home. I could only remember the way I felt—as if a slow and painful death was coming over me. You know how it feels when your parents whip you so bad that the stinging is so unbearable that your whole body gets a burning sensation until it reaches the state of numbness? The pain is so unfathomable that while you were crying, only tears would stream down your face and the wailings, screams, and groans were replaced by the jerking movements of your stomach muscles.

August 11, 2001
What was I going to do? In a few weeks I was going to visit my dad and stepmom in New York. I was wondering if there was anyway I could hide it from them. Oh God! Why is this happening to me?

How could Maoz let this happen? How could I be so stupid to believe him? How could I be so stupid to have sex with him? I was too young! Too young to get pregnant! I have to get rid of this. Oh God, let me fall down the steps! Please don't let this be true.

After I told Maoz the news, we both cried. He looked into my eyes and just said to me how sorry he was and that he knew that he would never see me again.

As I watched my mom get herself together after returning from work, she began to cook dinner. I struggled with myself, debating whether or not I should tell her or just keep it to myself and handle the problem.

How could I handle the problem? If I decide to get an abortion, which I will do, where would I get the money?

After hours of emotional torment, I sat my mother down for the first time of my life.

"Mom, I have something to tell you; it's very important." I looked into her eyes as she sat beside me on her bed, the same bed that I got pregnant on. I looked into her face; the words were too hard to share with her. For the first moment in my life my mom was there to listen, to understand. Her face was full of compassion and love for me.

"What's wrong, Lorna? Are you sick? Lorna…are you pregnant?"

"I don't know," I said, but I knew. I knew that the test was accurate. All the signs revealed it: the frequent trips to the bathroom in the morning and breasts that would leak. I remembered all the signs.

"Are you pregnant, Lorna?" She questioned me as if I was on trial.

"I don't know."

"I'll kill you, Lorna!" Again, death sounded so sweet when I was ten years old.

I have never seen my father cry the way he did except when his mother died. His whole body shook as he covered his face with his hand. The pain he felt reminisced in my mind. I remember seeing his hurt just a few weeks after I found out that I, at fifteen years old, was about to have a baby.

October 24, 2001
I crushed my mother's hopes and dreams for me. I remember sitting on the edge of the bed with her. I told her to sit down because I had something very important to tell her. This was the first time we ever spoke with each other like this.

I waited all day thinking of the right moment and the right words to tell her that her daughter had deceived her. Oh, my mother was so bright. We sat at the edge of the bed for what felt like an hour.

"What's wrong, Lorna? Are you sick?"

"No, I'm not sick."

Scene I: Now Name Your Destiny

"What's wrong, Lorna? (Pause) Are you pregnant?"

"I don't know." I knew that I was pregnant I just didn't didn't want to believe it.

"Oh, my God, Lorna, you're pregnant! Oh, my God, Lorna, I'll kill you! I'm going to go and tell your daddy right now!"

At that moment I wish she had killed me. I didn't want to continue living knowing that I hurt my parents and feeling as frightened as I did. I felt as if I fell in a black hole and there was no sign of light. There was no hope for me in this life. I was a failure! But twelve years later I would find that there was light in that black hole. All I had to do is open my eyes. My eyes were closed the whole time!

I lived in darkness most of my life wondering why I wasn't good enough. Why was I so ugly and lonely? Why did no one really love me? But the whole time I was being loved more than I could ever desire or imagine.

When my mother and father divorced and I grew up seeing other children's parents get involved in their school, and going to parent/teacher conferences, I felt different. I felt as though I was not a normal kid. My mother didn't understand a lot of English; therefore, she didn't want to get involved in any school activities that the other parents did.

I remembered my mom's boyfriend Edward. He was so good to her and me He never argued with her, and she was always so happy. Edward made my mom feel so secure. She didn't worry about bills or the house or him hurting her. Edward was so nice to me. He was the father I never had. I even called him daddy. He was the only other man that I would look at as a father besides my real dad. He was actually the only father that I knew. We were one happy family.

I remember when he came home with a puppy, I named him Tiny, but Edward called him Prince. Tiny was so cute. He was very small, with white fur and a few brown spots on his back that looked like a smiley face when he sat down. Tiny was like a little brother to me.

But that family would soon die just as the previous one. I never got the whole story as to why he left. My mother just told me that Edward's son was messed up and his ex-wife, his son's mother, would call all the time about her son. The next thing you know, Edward had left. My mom didn't want Edward's son to live with us in fear of his problem affecting the family and that he may hurt me. That was the second time my mother's heart had been broken.

My mom was such a beautiful lady with a kind heart just to have it broken over and over again. After her heart was torn the second time, she began to grow cold. She no longer wanted to be in a relationship based on love. Her past relationships, with the addition of the influence of her Thai friends, taught her to focus on survival. Men were only needed to assist in provision. You cannot rely on love because you will always get hurt! I did not want to believe that. I was still too young and was stuck on romance. I just wanted to be loved. My mom just wanted to survive. She never loved another man again.

I knew there was someone who would love me. Someone who would think I was pretty, smart, and special.

February 24, 2002
I spent my whole life keeping what I had done or what had been done to me just between God and myself. I thought I had forgiven my parents for hurting me, and all the men I was involved with for hurting me, but I forgot one person, myself. I was so bound by the shame of my past that I just wanted to keep it between God and me. I thought to myself, "I did my part." I asked God to forgive me for my sins, the hate, bitterness, and unforgiveness I had toward all of the people who had hurt me. But God had a different plan. He had a purpose for my life.

He told me:

"It is not about you or what happened to you and better yet who did it and why. It is about Me and what I have done to bring you out of that and what I am doing and going to do in your life.

"There are women out there who are waiting for you to tell them what I've done, and you are so busy trying to keep this between Me and you. There are women out there who are hurting, who are being abused right now.

Scene I: Now Name Your Destiny

"Do not walk in shame and guilt when I have already forgiven you. Share what I have done for you with others who are hurting the way you once did.

"It is not about you; it is all about Me. It is all about letting those women know that they are living in a lie. That they are believing in a lie. They have been lied to far too long, and now it is up to you to allow Me to use you.

"There is work that I have to do, and you are the vessel that I have chosen to use for this task. So allow Me to use you in order to do what is called to be done."

I was so caught up in trying to please everyone. I kept wondering why people would keep hurting me. I kept asking myself, "What is wrong with me? What have I done to cause people to hurt me like this?" I got to the point of being so exhausted with trying to please everyone by doing things I thought would make them love me. I didn't know who I was or what I wanted. I didn't even know what love was. I didn't even know how to love myself. Then I grew weary and stopped caring. I stopped trying to please my mom and dad or anyone else I cared about. I started walking in bitterness. Bitterness caused me to do all the things I did not believe in doing because I no longer believed in anything.

I started drinking at the age of seventeen. I had no stable home, and I left my son with one of his grandparents at any given time. I was going to clubs at that age and doing whatever else I wanted and considered fun. This ranged from smoking weed and partying to being sexually promiscuous.

I hung out with all the dealers and "gang bangers." It got to the point to where my life was a lie. I was empty inside. I couldn't recognize whether someone was loving me or using me, and most of the time they were doing the latter. But I felt I had it all under control because I was having this false sense of "fun."

I became that very same lie that I tried to avoid and hide. I hid my feelings by doing things that I thought would cover up my pain—the pain of an empty person searching for something that she felt she could never get and really didn't know much about, until the day that I found God. He became my shelter from the storm, my strength when I was weak, my comforter, my friend, my father, my mother, my lover, my deliverer, my all, my everything. Everything that I had searched for I found in Him, and it was genuine, and He told me it would be everlasting.

Regardless of how imperfect I was. I no longer had to prove myself to have the love that I had been searching for. To have the cold, dark hole inside of me filled. To get the high that I could never get from any joint or fifth of gin that all the money in the world could buy. His love was all I needed. His love is what I found.

February 26, 2002
God has been dealing with me for such a long time. You know I have gone through so many things. I have done so many things and so many things have been done to me. I kept pleading with God, "Please, let's just keep this between You and me. I don't want to hurt anyone by saying these things, and I don't want to keep reliving and replaying back those memories."

But He kept telling me, "Baby girl, I love you and I will protect you. I will comfort you, but know that it's not about those things that you've done. It's not about those things people have done to you.

"It's not about the physical abuse that you experienced when you were seventeen or the alcohol you would drink and then throw up just to fill up again. It's not about the drug abuse or the sexual promiscuity or the molestation. Do not be afraid, baby girl, because I love you.

"It is about how I healed you from all those things. It is about how I allowed you to love those people although they hurt you. It is about how I taught you how to love by first knowing what love looks like, what love truly is. I must use those things to let others know that I love them too regardless of what they have done, for My mercy endures forever. For I am Love.

"There's just too many of my daughters who are hurting or feel alone the way you did when you were young. Remember when you first felt this way at the age of ten? Remember at that age when you questioned Me, again, why you were created? It was part of My plan that only you could fulfill.

Scene I: Now Name Your Destiny

"I knew the enemy was going to speak lies to My daughters. I knew he was going to use the absence of their fathers in their lives in an effort to keep them searching for the loved they lacked from the world, searching to have a void filled that only I can truly fill.

"I want them to know that they no longer had to try to win daddy's love only to be left feeling unloved and unwanted because their fathers did not know how to give them the love they longed for. I want them to know that I can be the daddy they have longed for all their lives.

"I no longer want them throwing their hearts away to every man that they see, blinded by the abuse, not recognizing that the man they are with may be there for their destruction. I want them to give their hearts to Me so that I can keep them in a safe place away from harm as I give them that pure unconditional love.

"To heal their broken heart and to renew their minds so that I can prepare them for that man who knows Me. That man I have created for them that knows the love I have for My daughters and who I have prepared to love them like my daughters should be loved.

"Tell them how you drank when you were seventeen. How you would go into the liquor store with your friends and give them a few dollars to buy a pint of Mad Dog 20/20 as you would steal a fifth of gin that you were going to drink straight in attempts to fill the void you had inside. Tell them how proud you were of yourself that you had the ability to slide that tall bottle in the sleeve of your shirt and walk in a nonchalant manner thinking you did the owner a favor by buying a $3.00 dollar bottle of cheap wine. Oh yeah, you contributed all right.

"Tell them how you would drink that fifth all by yourself knowing you would be hugging the toilet in the next few hours until you would fall asleep.

"Tell them about the men you slept with. About how you dated one, and while he was with your friend at your mother's house, you were with his brother at their house sleeping with him, because you knew that your boyfriend was probably having sex with your friend.

"Tell them about all the men whose names you can't remember. Tell them about when you were nineteen and lost count of them, but you thought you were OK because you only slept with the man you were dating and you would date them for a long period of time, only to immediately jump into another relationship.

"Tell them how you slept with so many men corrupting the temple that I gave you so that you could continue to live a lie. You were living in shame only to do those things that would bring you more shame.

"Tell them how you left your son with his father's mother, or your mom or stepfather for so long that you don't even know what happened the majority of his first two years of his life.

"Tell them of all the perverted sexual acts you participated in. Tell them about the man you lived with when you were seventeen who physically abused you.

"How one day he threw you against a wooden couch breaking the back frame with your head. Then he threw your body against the wall and the floor. You still stayed with him even after he continued abusing you.

"He repeatedly hit you in your face, causing you to fall to your knees, and then kicked you in your ribs on your way down, leaving you with a bloody nose wondering if your ribs were broken.

"How this abuse caused you to be physical toward your own husband because any indication of physical altercation would bring fear in your heart. You were in fear of being an abused victim.

"The shame you felt by staying with someone who abused you because you felt you could help him. The control and manipulation he used toward you kept you in bondage.

"You were ashamed because you told one of your friends that was being abused by her boyfriend for so many years, 'Why are you letting that man hurt you like that?' But only a year after, you became a victim too.

"You were full of shame, so full of guilt, that you demonstrated it by never trusting a man again. You became defensive in fear of any man ever hitting you again so you would always attack first in the midst of any type of argument.

Scene I: Now Name Your Destiny

"Tell them about the shame you felt when you got molested at the age of twelve in an arcade spot that your mother told you not to go to. Then you saw him going into a Salvation Army van full of kids, keeping your mouth shut, not telling a word because you were afraid. Although you believed in your heart that some of those kids may be getting abused as well.

"How long will you continue to keep this between you and Me, My child? There's another little girl out there wondering why she is so unloved and unwanted. Remember how you first tried to take your life at the age of ten and then again when you were eighteen, soon after your son's father physically abused you, for the second time.

"You couldn't take it any more. You just left one situation, and then there goes the father of your only child jumping on your back when all you wanted was peace. So you took his mother's pills. A whole bottle of those pills she took because she had an anxiety problem. Tell them how he was so angry with you and scared for you for taking those pills. And the only way he knew how to show those feelings of fear was to call you stupid and by trying to kick you out of the car on the way to the hospital yelling at you, 'So you want to kill yourself? Let me help you!'

"Tell them how your mother reacted when she finally arrived at the emergency department. How she laughed at you in front of the nurses and doctors, telling them, 'Good, let her die.'

"She said those same words to you about your son Jerah when you were sixteen years old as you watched your son lay on the floor motionless, with a high grade fever, knowing your mom would not take him to the hospital. 'I'm not going to take that boy to the hospital and spend all my money! You see what happens when you're young and have a baby?' The hopelessness you felt as she told you, 'Good, let him die.'

"The words of a mother you loved so much. A mother bound by so much bitterness due to the betrayal she felt from those she loved. Words that came from a bitter heart full of anger, which continued to pierce your heart, only to cause your heart to become bitter as well.

" Tell them how you hated your mother for her lack of sympathy and how you heard her laughter ringing in your ears while you lay there wanting your life to end in that hospital bed as the nurses and doctors tried to force you to bring back up those pills you swallowed. Her laughter continued to resonate as its intensity grew, burning a hole in your heart.

"You were a liar, a thief, an alcoholic, a marijuana smoker, a promiscuous girl, a hater of life, living a lie, but I continued to love you. My love never changed for you.

"I continued to have mercy on you, and My grace kept you alive. I had my hands on you, and nothing was going to take your life. I tried to reach out to you, and you knew I was there, but My hands you would not take.

"You didn't think I cared because the enemy kept telling you that I was punishing you. That if I loved you I would not let you suffer like this. He kept telling you that you deserved the life you were in.

"But you kept praying through all those times, all of those days, through all of your mess, and I heard you every single time. I counted every single tear. But you couldn't see Me. You could only see your mess.

"You were blinded by a lie that no one loved you or wanted you. I always loved and wanted you even before I created the world. Then when I created you, it was only you that would complete and fulfill a purpose to share the very same thing that you would want to keep just between you and Me but would be shared to deliver others.

"It is time to let them know that I am here for them and that I love them. No matter what they've done or what was done to them, I love them.

They are My children, and they are beautiful. I have died so that they may have life and life more abundantly. My unconditional love is what they are searching for and what they need to make them complete in order to fill their emptiness and mend their hearts. I can even teach them to love their enemies as I have taught you.

"So what will it be? Will you allow yourself to be available for Me? Don't worry about your ability or what I have planned or how I am going to do it, just allow Me to use you. You were chosen for this.

"You are a blessing, My precious daughter. I will comfort you and protect you all the days of your life. Hold My hand, and I will lift you up above all your enemies.

"Are you ready? Because I have been waiting."

I am ready, Father.

LETTER #1 TO MY DADDY

Dear Daddy,
I remember when I was about five years old and you picked me up to spend time with you. You took me to a woman's apartment. I thought you stayed there because there was a painting of me when I was a baby hanging on her living room wall.

I was wearing a yellow dress and my hair was combed and styled naturally, showing all my curls. It was a beautiful painting. I wonder where it is now. If I'd ask you, would you even tell me the truth? I wonder. How could you take me to a place, to that woman's apartment who you were with while you were still married to my mom?

I remember you taking me back home. I told my mom about the woman and her apartment. My mom asked me if I could take her there, if I could remember how to get to her apartment. I told her that I remembered and I showed her the way. I remembered my mom knocking on the door as I was standing beside her, waiting for someone to answer. When that other woman opened the door, my mom immediately started asking her questions.

You hurt my mom and you hurt me. How could you do something like that? I was so young, but you still lied to me. What makes me think that you wouldn't lie to me now?

That woman was also a liar. The two of you belonged together. "Birds of a feather..." She told Mom how you were not there, that you were out fishing with her husband. Mom was too smart to believe her. Mom knew she was lying and let the other woman know it. Mom was never the one to keep her mouth shut. "I don't believe you. I know my husband is here!" I don't know exactly what the other woman said, but she tried her hardest to stick to that same lie. Liar, my dad never went fishing!

As my mom and that lady continued exchanging words, I went into the apartment looking for you. I knew you were in there. I could remember your face as if it were yesterday. You were sitting on a bed with your glasses on, smoking a cigarette. You placed a finger to your lips to notion me to "Shh." That was it! "Mom!" I yelled. "Daddy is in the room smoking a cigarette!" I knew then that my father was sneaky, a liar, and most of all a cheat. My mom kept talking about how good I remembered where you were and other things about you. I can't remember, but I am sure it wasn't nice things.

After that incident, I do not remember your presence. Except when we returned from New York for Christmas, but that happened before you decided to be with another woman, or did it? Oh, I also remember the time you came to visit with your stepmother Mary. You were never around, and I hated you for that. You made me feel like you didn't care. How could you have left my mom and me? You were never there physically, but your sins and the pain you left lingered and followed us everywhere we went. My mother was angry with you, and because you were not there, I had to take the punishment you deserved. She saw you in me, and I had to pay for that.

I was lonely and you were not there. You found it more important to be with other women and to go out to the clubs and smoke and drink than to be with us. I felt betrayed, worthless, and lonely. I never trusted men, and I always felt they would leave, and they did every time. Or I would leave them before they got the chance.

I can remember a vision that I approached you with once before. I was standing at the top of the stairs and you and Mom were on the couch. You were on top of her hitting her. I remember blood, a lot of blood coming out of her ears. When I asked you about this horrible vision, you cussed at me. Was that to cover up some of the truth that lied in that vision that you hurt my mom not only mentally but physically as well? Why would that nightmare keep visiting me, even while I was awake?

I love you with all my heart, but I can't keep chasing you. It hurts me to be fifteen minutes away, and you don't call or visit the kids or me. I feel rejected. I feel that you are avoiding all the issues that we have. You do not want to speak to me about anything that is meaningful.

You are avoiding being a father to me, and I am angry. I feel that you do not love me but choose to love other women more, the way you did years ago. I am angry and hurt. But I still love you. I am hurt, and only the Lord can help me to forgive you. I want you in my life, but I will no longer chase you. I have got to say good-bye. Good-bye to the past. Good-bye to the pain and anger. Good-bye to the bitterness. I do not have any time to be burdened by the past. The Lord needs me, and I have to make myself available to Him now.

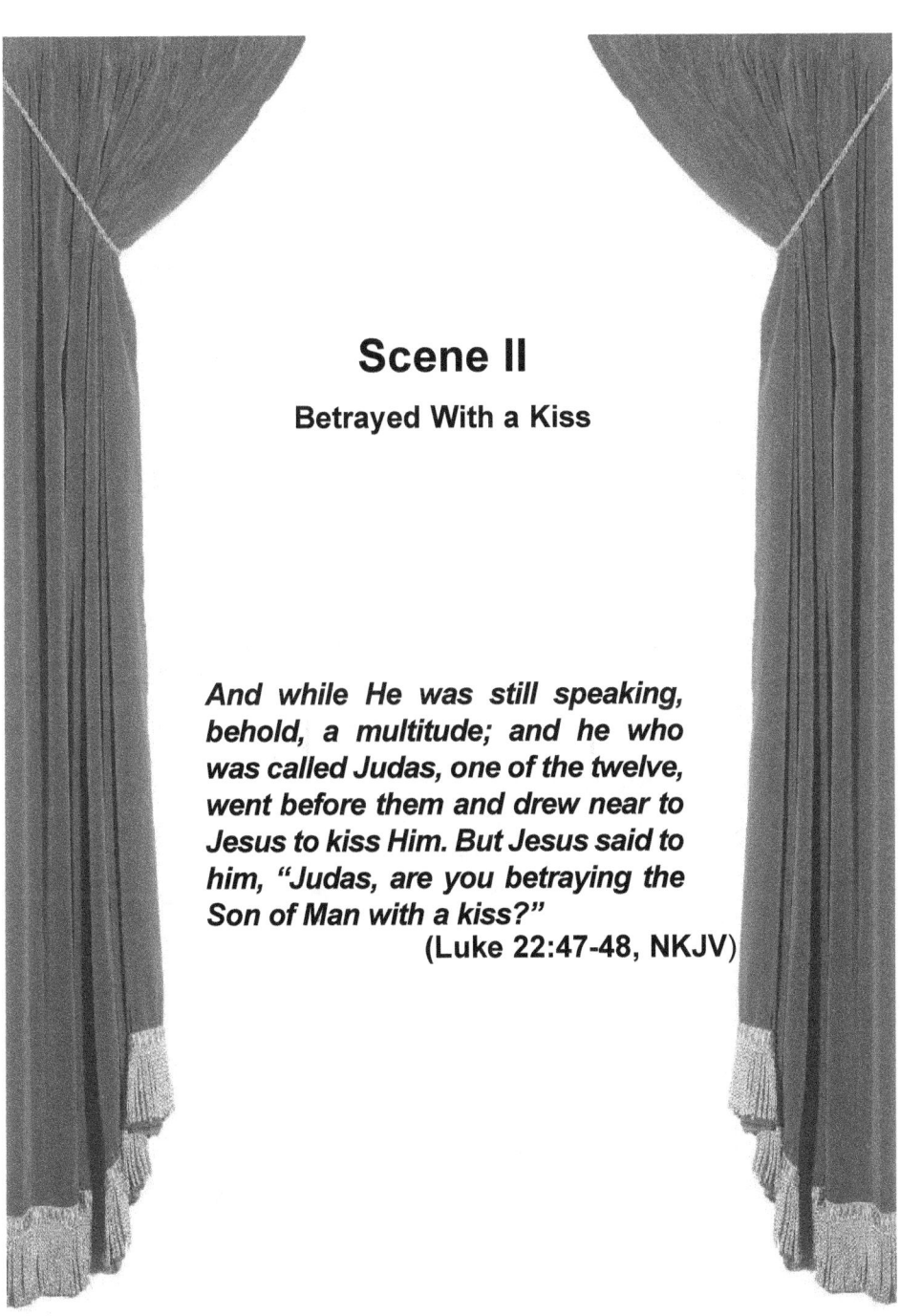

Scene II

Betrayed With a Kiss

And while He was still speaking, behold, a multitude; and he who was called Judas, one of the twelve, went before them and drew near to Jesus to kiss Him. But Jesus said to him, "Judas, are you betraying the Son of Man with a kiss?"
          (Luke 22:47-48, NKJV)

Destiny, formerly known as Lorna, was already walking in the purpose God had for her life. Although she knew her purpose, she still had to receive the revelation of who she was in Christ.

It was the summer of 2002, and Destiny found herself yet again in another ungodly relationship. God had to remind her of the Judases in her life. God asked her a very important question: "When will you seek Me and realize that I am the only true love that could ever fulfill all your needs? As long as you seek fulfillment in man you will continue to find yourself in the cycle of ungodly and unhealthy relationships."

THE JUDASES IN MY LIFE

When some of us think back about Judas and what he had done, our hearts get filled with anger. But for those who sit back and see the whole picture, we thank God that Judas was the traitor that he was. Praise God for the Judas in the world and the enemies in our lives, for they are the ones who push us into our destiny.

Dealing with the emotional aspect of being a single mother at the age of fifteen wasn't very easy, especially when you really couldn't figure out how you got yourself in this mess in the first place. Sex is just a minute factor that assisted in the end result, but the reality was in the answer to the question, Why would I have sex at the age of fifteen? What was I looking for that I thought I could get by having sex with this person? This was one of the few behaviors I displayed that demonstrated I was looking for love in all the wrong places. In my journey I tried to find it in places, through other people, and in things.

At the age of seventeen, I had found myself going to clubs, being sexually promiscuous, and an alcoholic. I wanted to know where could I find this thing called love. How could I get a piece of it so that the feelings of loneliness and low self-worth would disappear? I was curious and determined to find the answer, but like they say, "curiosity killed the cat." It almost killed me several times, but fortunately I had more than nine lives. I had the grace of God on me every step of the way.

But he said to me, "My grace is sufficient for you, for my power is made perfect in weakness." Therefore I will boast all the more gladly about my weaknesses, so that Christ's power may rest on me.

(2 Corinthians 12:9, NIV)

THE FIRST JUDAS

Yanna was cool to hang out with. We would chill to some music, play some cards with the fellas, and drink until we were drunk.

I knew he had dated Bernadette, my former best friend, but Yanna and I were just friends. But for some reason, Bernadette wasn't "feelin'" that. One night while Yanna and I were at his house in our regular routine of chillin' out, Bernadette decided to pay us a little visit. Needless to say it wasn't a friendly one. Bernadette was out in the street cursing and yelling for me to come outside. Yanna and I climbed the basement stairs, trying to maintain our unstable balance due to the toxins flowing through our veins, to see what was going on in the streets. The closer we got to the top of the stairs we realized that it was Bernadette.

She was out there infuriated with the two of us. I knew that she wanted to fight me. I wasn't ready to fight in the state that I was in, nor did I have the courage to. I kept trying to explain to her the truth about Yanna and I only being friends, but she wasn't buying that. Who would have blamed her anyway?

You learned that you do not date or mess around with any of your friends' or even former friends' boyfriends. This was totally disrespectful. Bernadette felt I had disrespected her and was pissed off about it. She was so enraged that she wanted to release all of her frustrations out on me. Little did Bernadette know that her false accusations would lead to Yanna and me becoming a couple. I now dated the ex-boyfriend of a new enemy.

I think I was about sixteen or seventeen the first time I ever moved in with a guy who had his own place. It was a small four-room apartment consisting of one bedroom, one bathroom, one kitchen, and a liv-

Scene II: Betrayed With a Kiss

ing room, but the idea of doing whatever you wanted whenever you wanted sounded real good to me at the time. It sounded real good until I started to see that I was sleeping with the enemy.

One day at Yanna's parents' house I ran into one of Yanna's ex-girlfriends, who was now Yanna's sister's best friend. She shared her experience with dating Yanna.

She told me how Yanna tried to throw her down the steps one day because he got so angry at her during an argument they had. I was really shocked to hear anything about Yanna like that since I had not experienced or witnessed it personally, until this one particular day.

Between Yanna and me, I was the only one who had a car, and since I called myself "in love," I didn't have a problem sharing it with him. So one day while I was driving myself to school with Yanna in the passenger seat, so he could take the car that day, we got into an argument. I was complaining to him about the holes he had made in my car in order to install some speakers. My mom saw the holes and jumped all over me about it, which didn't help our broken-up mother-daughter relationship.

She bought me the car a year ago, and now it was getting torn up and I was getting yelled at for something that I didn't do and I was going to let Yanna know how I felt about it. I was so furious about the way he was tearing up my car and more so because he was doing that stupid laugh while I was being serious that I decided to use the car to get back at him. I told him that I wasn't going to let him use the car and that he would have to walk back home. He laughed it off with that crazy laugh he always did when he felt that I was just "trippin'," you know, "She's just a little upset, but she'll get over it. I'll make it up to her and she'll forget all about it." But this time I decided to prove him wrong. I was going to let him know that I meant business. He thought I was joking, so he continued to laugh it off until I parked the car in the school parking lot, turned off the car, took the key, and started getting out of the car. As soon as I closed the door, Yanna had already made his way in front of me, blocking me from leaving.

I am not sure what I said word for word, but I think it was something to the fact of him letting me go so that I could go in. I was late for school, so there was no one in the parking lot except Yanna and me, well at least that's what I thought. He immediately threw me against the car door with so much force that I thought I was going to end up back in the car through the car door. He was yelling at me and cursing at me to get back in the car.

Fear suddenly filled my stomach, along with more anger, but because I had to be tough, I refused his command. He threw me against the car door a few more times, letting me know that the tough act wasn't going to work. Sometimes we think we just get lucky, but as I sit back and write these words, replaying those memories of that bright, warm, spring school day morning, now knowing who God is and how He protects us, I know that He sent an angel to help me.

> *For he shall give his angels charge over thee, to keep thee in all thy ways.*
>
> (Psalm 91:11, KJV)

From out of nowhere came a student that I had never seen before. I don't know what he was doing out in the parking lot or where he came from, but he saved me from an unimaginable fate. The stranger asked me if I was OK and told Yanna to chill out. I don't remember what was said at that point, but all I remember doing was jumping in my car and driving to Yanna's apartment as fast as I possibly could.

As tears streamed down my cheeks from the fright of what just happened, all I could think about was getting my things out of his place.

Once I arrived at his apartment, I started grabbing everything that belonged to Jerah and me. I was in such a frantic stage that I was not sure if I was going in circles or actually putting things in my car. I probably made six or seven trips to the car, praying that this nightmare would soon end.

While making one of my trips out to the car, there to greet me was my enemy. Yanna had to have run all the way from the high school to the apartment. Regardless of how he got there in such a short amount of time, he was there, and he was standing right in

Scene II: Betrayed With a Kiss

front of me, blocking me from going out the door. The last words I could remember were, "Where the h-ll do you think you're going?"

As I sat back with my bruised and broken body, I thought of my friend Khara. Khara was a beautiful girl around my same age, around sixteen or seventeen. She had been in an abusive relationship for as long as I could remember. How could anyone that young, beautiful, and smart stay with a boyfriend who would beat her up on a routine basis?

Her boyfriend Tamar had seen his father beat up his mother all his life. He hated his father for abusing his mother and his mother more for allowing his father to do it. Who would have known that the person he hated the most, he would turn out to be like, and the woman he hated more for taking the abuse, he had turned Khara into. Although their arguments would cause him to get physical with her, she still chose to argue with him. I remember the time they were in my car. Khara was sitting in the front seat with me while I was driving, and Tamar was sitting in the back right behind Khara. Like always, they started arguing. I was just thinking to myself, "Please don't start this in my car, because I don't want to see them fighting and don't want to see Khara getting beat up."

The argument escalated, and Tamar started getting physical. I remember him kicking Khara in the back of her head over and over again. I kept yelling at him to stop fighting in my car. He kept calling Khara stupid, and she kept saying something back to him that made him kick her in the back of her head again. I would always ask her, "Why do you let him hit you like that? Why don't you just break up with him? I would never let anyone kick my a— like that."

Now I sat back seeing myself being thrown into the wall over and over, then slammed onto the part of the floor that had no carpet. "You want to leave me, huh? You're not going anywhere. You better not leave me." Through all my screams, cries, and pleading, Yanna kept repeating this over and over while throwing me around. He kept asking me if I wanted to leave, and I answered that I would never leave. "You better not ever leave me," he said as he picked me up from the floor and threw me against the wooden frame of the couch in his little four-room apartment.

"How could you stay with someone who beats you up all the time?" Now I knew why Khara stayed...you tell yourself they love you; they didn't mean it; it won't happen again; I just have to be a little more understanding; I can't leave; they need me; I should have never made him mad in the first place, and it was all my fault." Truth be told, you stay because you don't realize just how valuable you are in God's eyes. You stay because you were taught by watching others that relationships are supposed to be like this. These are all lies that the enemy has told you to keep your family, and every generation that follows, living in the curse of abuse.

I never knew my body could take so much abuse. No broken bones, just a sore head that felt like it was split open and a body full of bruises. As I lay there on the bed with my bloodshot eyes and cheeks stained by the salt of the tears that once ran down my face, this man that I loved, the man that I freely gave myself to was pleading with me to forgive him, telling me that he was so sorry, that he didn't want to lose me, and to never leave him. He promised me that he would never hurt me again, and I told him that I would not leave. Maybe I can help him or change him. If he said he wouldn't hurt me again, he probably wouldn't. But something deep down inside told me I'd better not try to leave, that my body may not survive the next round. It's amazing how much pressure a rubber band can take before it pops...

It had been a few months since I experienced the wrath of a desperate lover. Everything seemed to be going well. We would argue occasionally, but I would never argue with him to the point of causing him to get out of control again.

I would look at the broken slab of wood on the back of the couch and remember the pain my head felt as it was used as a sledge hammer; the memory alone caused me to curl up like a fetus in its mother's womb. I would immediately drop my "tough" act, knowing that Yanna was a lot tougher. He acted as if nothing had ever happened that bright, warm, spring, school-day morning that turned into one of the many darkest days of my life and just one of the few with Yanna.

Suddenly there was a knock at the door. Yanna looked at me and started toward the door. It was Maoz, my son's father, and his cousin

Scene II: Betrayed With a Kiss

they called Ach. Yanna went to answer the door. I barely heard their brief conversation, then Yanna walked toward me and then past me with this disgusted look on his face. The look said, "Don't start with me," as he mumbled that Maoz was there to see me.

As I walked toward the door I saw Maoz and his cousin Ach. Ach and Maoz both had a Rottweiter puppy. They were also wearing their infamous Los Angeles Raiders caps with the brims cut off. This so-called fad began the perpetrating of gangs in our high school, but then the perpetrating became reality. Our little town now consisted of two gangs, the Bloods and the Cripps. Although they were not allowed to wear those caps in school anymore, it didn't stop them from wearing them out on the streets. Maoz, Ach, and I made our way to the side of our apartment, which was a part of a small strip of property divided into three apartments.

Luckily Yanna and I stayed in the apartment on the end; it gave us more privacy. Maybe Yanna was lucky in this aspect since it would allow him to use me as a "punching bag" without anyone knowing, but I think a lot of people knew but just didn't say anything. I actually preferred it that way so I wouldn't feel as embarrassed knowing that everyone knew I was sleeping with a guy who almost brought me close to death. I didn't want anyone to let me know how stupid they thought I was. They wouldn't understand. They didn't see the Yanna that I did. He really wasn't all that bad. He just needs a little love, a little attention, and someone who understands. I felt that I had to be the one to help him, although it may cost me my life, but for some reason I really believed that he was sorry and that it wouldn't happen again.

"What's up, Shorty?" Maoz asked.

"Not much. Just chillin'. What's up with you and Ach? I like your puppies; they're cute." I replied.

Maoz just looked at me and jumped right into this interrogation mode. I could tell he was not there for any small talk. "Maannnn, what's up, Shorty? Why you with this nigga? I know he's beating you up. You need to wake up and smell the coffee, girl, before he really hurts you," Maoz said.

"You know, I don't know why you girls trip. You let these guys beat you, and then you still stay with them. You know Ezriella could whip all kinds of girls, but that little boyfriend she's with, she let's him abuse her!" exclaimed Ach.

I remembered the day that Ezriella got into a fight in middle school with some very tough girls, and she could hold her own, most definitely. She ended up getting her shirt torn off of her, but that girl was throwin' down. Then I thought about her puny little boyfriend and could not believe that he was beating her up. Yanna was twice my size, and if I dared to fight back, he would probably kill me for real.

Maoz and Ach kept going on and questioning why I stayed with Yanna. I remembered the time Maoz and I got into a fight. I punched him in his groin area and he took my arm and twisted it to my back the way a police officer would do to restrain an aggressive person. Afterward I basically broke off the relationship and told him off. All that drama because he thought I was messing around with someone else. Now he's here trying to judge me. Pleease!

Maoz and Ach continued to go on and on about how stupid I was, and then Maoz started telling me about Yanna and his ex-girlfriend riding around in my car and that everyone knew it except for me. Well, if that didn't break the straw on the camel's back! I remember that expression when I told a family member that she was nosy, although I was telling the truth.

Suddenly I felt this deep pain in my stomach, like a burning sensation you get when you take your final exam, knowing your grade would determine whether or not you graduated. The pain I felt when I found out I was pregnant at the age of fifteen.

Oh, I was really pissed, and Maoz knew it. He knew exactly what it would take to get me mad, and that's why he was there. If I wasn't going to be with him, then he didn't want anyone else to be with me either. Since the abuse was not keeping me from Yanna, he figured telling me about him being with some other girl would do the trick, especially a girl that Yanna used to date. He was right. I was ready to go back into that little apartment and tell him off. How dare he ride some girl in my car while I was at school?

Scene II: Betrayed With a Kiss

At that point Maoz knew he accomplished what he set out to do, so he was ready to go home, which was right around the corner. I knew some stuff was about to hit the fan. There was definitely going to be some "drama for your mamma," and I didn't care how bad it got. As I made my way through the door with my stomach feeling like I drank a whole bottle of grain alcohol I was thinking about how bad I was going to cuss this guy out.

I sat on the edge of the bed directly across from the only dresser we had since only one would fit in that tiny room. He came over and sat on the dresser directly across from me. Yanna knew I was pissed off and was very curious to know what Maoz had to say. I skipped over the remarks about everyone knowing that Yanna beating me up and went directly to the chase. "Maoz told me that you've been messing around with your old girlfriend and that you were riding her around in my car while I was in school."

"He's lying," Yanna answered.

"Well, I don't believe you. Why would he lie to me about that?" I snapped back.

"I don't know, but I'm not messing around with her. We're just friends, and I may have given her a ride once, but I don't always ride her around in your car. Do you believe him?" he asked.

I thought to myself, What kind of question is that? If I didn't believe him, then why would I tell you that I don't believe you?

I looked at Yanna dead in his eyes and saw the fury in his eyes, but I didn't care. I wanted him to know that I was not going to let him mess around on me. As we stared into one another's eyes, he asked me the question again, but this time slower, making sure I understood the question. "Do you believe him?"

"Yes," I replied wearing a straight face like a wedding couple giving their "I Dos."

As soon as the "s" completely fell from my lips and began echoing in the air, Yanna drew his arm back with the back of his hand curved. As I look at all the veins protruding from his long and narrow fingers down his forearm wrapping around his arm all the way down to his elbow, I thought to myself that this must be a threat just to make me give him the answer he wanted.

As soon as my eyes made their way back to look into his eyes, which were fierce as fire, like a lion ready to attack his enemy trying to intrude on his territory, Yanna brought his hand down and back-slapped me. Immediately I felt a sting so painful that my whole right side felt numb. I could see stars as they floated in midair above my eyes like a cloud of fairy-tale dust. My ears began ringing and throbbing. I was not sure if my teeth were still intact and whether my eyes would swell up like an injured boxer now on the tenth round.

Although the pain was more than I could have ever imagined, Yanna continued to ask me the question, "Do you believe him?" With every question my stubbornness would not allow any answer except "Yes." But the question was no longer a question but some sort of cadence call. When I ask you, "Do you believe him?" you say "No." Being the strong-willed person that I was, I refused to give in. Now I can see that some of my daughter's strong personality and willpower is from me as well as her father. I would paddle her behind, but she would refuse to be obedient. I guess she felt I would give in and let her get her way. I would eventually end up being merciful.

But Yanna did not have the same love and mercy that a parent has for their child or even a lover would have toward their mate. No, he was led by power and power alone. If I did not cower to his commands, then he would force me to do so even if it meant beating it in me. The only memories of parenting he reminded me of was the infamous saying, "I brought you into this world and I will take you out!" I knew that he had no part of bringing me into the world, but I had no doubt in my mind that he had the power to take me out.

Each time I told Yanna that I believed the rumors Maoz was so nice to let me in on, I would feel the power of his wrath. The magnitude of each mighty blow caused after the third or fourth strike caused numbness to my head. I felt the drunkenness of a homeless man stumbling the streets with his bottle of whisky concealed in a brown bag now only left with a swig of his happy juice. His stammering words begging for another dollar in hopes to contribute to

Scene II: Betrayed With a Kiss

the only world he wants to know, a world without any memories of his failures or thoughts of an empty tomorrow.

As the room was spinning, I felt as if I were in a trance. The only word that I knew how to say at this point was "Yes." Yes, I believe you are a dirty dog. Yes, I believe you had her in my car that I graciously allowed you to use while I was in school. Yes, yes, yes!

With the last blow to my face, I could no longer keep my balance. I felt a warm ooze seep from out of my nostrils as my balance gave out. At that point gravity had won; it was stronger than my will. My body began its way to the floor, but before my knees could hit the matted-down carpet, his knee met my ribs. As the force of his block caused my body to fall to the side, I discovered that the warmth coming from my nose was a thick crimson substance. He had slapped me so many times that my nose started to bleed, and now the evidence ran down my face and onto my shirt.

As I struggled to stand on my feet I stumbled into the bathroom only a few steps away. At this point I had not known the severity of the facial beating I had just endured. Yanna's words echoed in the background due to the ringing in my ears. I grabbed the edge of the sink with my head now heavy, facing the white porcelain bowl with its ring of rust surrounding the drain. Drops of blood fell from my face, making its way down the drain. I lifted my head up slowly, afraid of seeing the condition my face would be in. As I looked at myself in the mirror, slowly turning my face side to side, inspecting the craftiness in the hands of an artist whose first love was abuse.

There were no trace of scratches or even bruises that would turn that deep royal blue and black color you could sometimes see late at night overlooking the area that the sun had just set hours ago. In addition to the swelling on the left side of my face were the scarlet outlines of the blood. The blood that once flowed from my nose that ran down my lips and chin, making its way freely to wherever gravity pulled it.

As the ringing of my ears started to subside, Yanna's words were becoming more understandable, yet still faint. He was saying something to the effect that I made him do it. "See what you made me do?" I wasn't quite sure, but I had heard it before after the incident with the car. As he was walking toward me, my body started to get stiff. It was the feeling you get while you're dreaming that you're falling down a cliff. You get very stiff for a moment, and then as soon as you start feeling your body making its journey down this long canyon with no visible end, you jump up, rescuing yourself. As his body surfaced the back of mine, he wrapped his arms around me.

"I'm sorry, Boo. I told you that I'm not messing around. I don't want anyone else but you. But you won't believe me." As his meaningless and insincere apologies danced in my head I knew I had to get out of there.

"I have to go to Maoz's house," I said.

"You're not going anywhere!"

I knew he wouldn't want me out of his sight until he knew for sure that there was no evidence to reveal what had just taken place. "I told Maoz that I would go over there and get Jerah. If I don't go over there, he's going to come back over here." Well, Yanna definitely didn't want that to happen.

"Go ahead and get Jerah and hurry up! You know I love you, Boo," he reminded me as his tone shifted from cruel to compassionate.

I washed my face with cool water, hoping the swelling and redness would go down. I also tried to clean up any traces of blood that I could find. I stood there for a moment trying to get my body to stop shaking. I walked around the corner and made my way toward. Maoz's closed-in porch. I controlled my shaky hand enough to open the first screen door, which eventually led to another one leading to the house. I successfully made it to the second door without shedding any tears or having any violent shakes.

Theresa, Maoz's sister answered the door and looked at me. A deep sympathetic look came over her. "Oh, my God, Lorna, what happened?" I couldn't hold the tears back any longer, nor could my body keep its limp state that I had placed it in so the shaking would stop. As the streams of tears rolled down my face, my body just burst. It felt like I was a balloon popping. My mouth opened and my lungs gave in as I released a powerful cry I could no longer sustain.

Scene II: Betrayed With a Kiss

"Maoz, come in here quick. Lorna got hurt!" Theresa commanded Maoz. I heard Maoz and Ach running from the back as Maoz's mom Eema slowly trailed behind, which was actually faster than I had ever seen her move. I heard him yell something as he turned the corner and took his first glance at me. It was the first time I had seen Maoz with so much anger. So much anger, yet so much compassion! He was a soldier in the army and the enemy just shot his best friend. As he looked at his friend slowly dying a painful death, the hunger of revenge consumed his heart and filled his mind of ideas on how to make the enemy suffer. This was like a soldier with thoughts of cutting each limb off the enemy, while watching him in pain, hoping to satisfy his loss.

"What did he do to you?" I tried to give an explanation, but each word that came out of my mouth was followed by an uncontrollable jerk. My lips were filled with tears that would fall from my mouth as soon as they made their way inside it. "Call the police, Mom!" Maoz shouted.

"No, please, Eema, don't call the police!" I pleaded.

"Mom, call the police now!" Maoz once again commanded but with more sternness. I knew that he had won that battle. Eema always listened to Maoz even when he would act up, which was usually the case. I remember always being there to help her win the battles against Maoz. I was her shield, the protector of her rights that Maoz would always try to disrespect.

"I'm going over there and I'm going to kill him! Come on, Ach!" Maoz shouted. I yelled at Maoz to stop and not go over there, but I knew he wouldn't listen. When anger filled his heart and revenge flowed through his veins, no boundaries or walls could contain him. I was thinking, "Let him go so he could kill him," but my heart was feeling another thing. It was feeling the pain that I might endure after Maoz had his turn because after Maoz, Yanna would have his turn with me again. There was also a feeling of sympathy toward Yanna.

"Just leave him alone!" I thought to myself. But my empty pleas meant nothing to Maoz. Besides, Maoz and Ach already made their way through the screen door. Eema was on the phone talking to someone from the police department, and Theresa went back to watching television. Theresa really wasn't the type of person to console you, but I could see her pain for me as she watched the tube.

I slumped down on the couch that was in the room adjacent to the living room and kitchen. There were no walls there, just a big opening that made the house appear bigger. As the tears started to stop flowing and the shaking ceased, I felt a brief moment of peace.

It seemed as if hours had passed since Maoz and Ach left, but it had only been minutes. Suddenly the screen door opened, immediately followed by the house door. My body jumped at the sound of the door slamming back. Before the screen door closed, Ach and Maoz were back in the house.

They were cussing about Yanna as they walked toward me. They were so pumped up that they probably would have fought anyone who even glanced at them the wrong way.

"He didn't open the door, 'cause he knew he was going to get his a— kicked! Mom, did you call the police?" Maoz said without taking a breath between each sentence.

"Yes, Maoz, they're on their way over here."

"What happened?" Maoz asked. This time he was interested in knowing the details. I explained to him how I confronted Yanna about his ex and how he kept slapping me because I told him that I believed Maoz and not him.

Yanna was arrested for assaulting a minor. The police officer encouraged me to get my belongings, get out, and not to come back. They didn't know how long Yanna was going to be incarcerated. This time I packed everything in the car, not leaving a single dish. The first time I only wanted the major things, but this time I would take it all, not leaving Yanna with anything that belonged to me. Most of the things we had belonged to me except the furniture, which belonged to the landlord.

My heart boiled over with hate as I was loading up the car. Not only did Yanna do this to me again, breaking his promise that I foolishly believed, but now I had to go back home and stay with my mom who I did not get along with. We had not gotten along since the day I stepped foot off that little crop duster plane, returning from Delaware. I remember my clothes being covered with Jerah's vomit. God, I wish I was back there with Chana, Magen, Davona, and Jonathan. We made such an awesome family, so why did Chana send me back here? I had told her that my mom did not want me anymore, but Chana explained that she couldn't live with herself knowing that she may have denied my mother and I a chance to have a good relationship together, even if I was sixteen with a baby.

I begged and pleaded with Chana as tears filled my eyes, but she was tough. She had to let me go. She had to give my mother and me a chance. Oh God, how I wished she were selfish, just for that one time. But her unselfishness made Chana the beautiful person that she was. For the very first time, I felt like I was a part of a family, something I wanted my whole life, and now it was being taken away from me again.

I went to the bed that was used as the source of the recent shock therapy I had just received. I started removing the comforter and then the sheets. Once I got to the head of the bed, I reached underneath the mattress to grab the tightly tucked in sheet. As my hand journeyed under the mattress, it discovered some sort of hard object. My hand stopped moving as I thought to myself, "Did I hide something under the mattress?" I lifted up the mattress slowly, peeking inside the way a child does as he lifts the lid from the cookie jar in anticipation of a wonderfully sweet, crunchy, or chewy treat.

My heart suddenly skipped a beat. The stars I saw floating around like fairy-tale dust now danced in my stomach. I gazed at the sharp object with its black handle in amazement. I had never felt that under the bed before, nor could I recall a time that I may have hidden it there. Yanna must have put it there today after I went to Maoz's house. I stared at the ten-inch butcher knife, imagining the thrusts it would have made as it penetrated my flesh. With every deadly jab I would have pleaded with my tears and my cries as my enemy watched me begging for his mercy. He would have the power to save my life. He would have watched me with the eyes of a demonically possessed person.

I thought about the newspaper article I read about my cousin's tragic death. Her boyfriend stabbed her several times, leaving her to slowly drown in a pool of water and blood as he left her there to die in her own waterbed. She screamed for help but no one came. No one tried to stop that mad man. My aunt let me read the poem my cousin had written describing this unimaginable death. Did she know she was to endure a fate that would cause her so much pain, so much sorrow? As she watched and felt the countless attacks from a man she once loved? He was her friend, her lover, and her confidant.

After reading her poem, it created a fear in me to not write any of my horrifying visions or dreams, afraid that the pencil would write them into existence. There were dreams of loved ones being taken away and the attempts to rescue them failed. The last look you see on their face, a look of hopelessness that haunts you even when you're already awake. Left condemned by guilt that you didn't try hard enough to save them. I still recall this dream I had when I was fifteen. I was running after this moving van or bus the kidnapper had my baby brother in. I was running as fast as I could to catch up, but the faster I ran, the faster the automobile traveled. I remember my brother's face, sad and innocent as he waved his final good-bye.

I sat at the corner of the bed with the hunter's dagger in my hand. I was going to be his prey. He would wait for me to walk through that front door, and then he'd have his way with me. He would have complete power over me. The power I gave up the first time I decided to stay. The first time I decided that he needed help and that I would be that chosen person.

In every relationship all parties have decisions to make. We all have choices. Although the choices we make may not be wise ones, they are our choices. And with those decisions there are consequences. Depending on who you believe you are, which is usually based on your past experiences or what people have told you, this will have a deep impact on the choices you make.

Insecure people who have a past history of rejection or some form of abuse will usually base their decision in either one of these ways. They may decide to avoid the situation or relationships altogether in order to avoid being rejected anymore, or they will decide to choose ways that they feel would give them control of the situation where they become manipulative.

Scene II: Betrayed With a Kiss

When there are two insecure people in a relationship, in which most times is the case since an insecure person tends to get into relationship with another insecure person, the relationship will be very dysfunctional. This relationship will lack trust and have one or both parties trying to control and manipulate the other. I thought that I could control the situation by giving Yanna everything he wanted. I used my material possessions along with sex as a form of manipulation. Yanna, on the other hand, was trying to control me with his physical power. If I stepped out of line, he would gladly get me back on track. Although it would cause me pain.

It was necessary in order for him to maintain the upper hand. I made the choice to give him power over my body, my mind, and my emotions, and I was too insecure to realize that I had the power to take it back. So I once again chose to turn back and walk the path that I had just left. Yanna was visiting with me at my mother's house. I am not sure how long it had been since my last experience with this enemy of mine, but again I chose to play on the enemy's playground.

Since our last bout, Yanna had gotten into a fight with one of my friends; this time it happened to be a guy. Migdal and I grew up together. He was Thai and African American like me, and our mothers knew each other. Our mothers were like sisters and would help one another. I was surprised to see Yanna fighting with another male, especially when I only heard about him fighting his girlfriends, and to make matters worst, to get into a fight with Migdal. I remember Yanna trying to avoid fighting Migdal because he knew Migdal would win.

Regardless, when Migdal wanted to fight, you were going to fight one way or another, and Migdal tore Yanna up! Yanna's retaliation only caused him to get more battered. With every return hit, Yanna's knuckles scrapped the concrete. His own blood covered his hands. Migdal, on the other hand, left without a single mark. I don't even think there was a bead of sweat that excreted from Migdal's body.

I believe I was dusting my mother's dining room table having a conversation with Yanna. He had his injured hand on the table with his knuckles bandaged the way a boxer would tape his hand up before sliding his hands into his gloves. Being the clumsy person that I was, I accidentally brushed the surface of his injured knuckles. Yanna quickly jerked his hand to his chest in order to soothe the throbbing pain I had just caused. As I was saying I was sorry, Yanna took the same elbow attached to his injured hand and drew it back.

His elbow made full contact with one of my eyes, immediately causing it to tear uncontrollably. While I cupped my eye with my hands, Yanna returned to nurturing his knuckles. He played it off as if he didn't know what he had just done. Sure, it is a natural reflex to elbow someone who touches a sore part of your hand. I accidentally hurt Yanna, but he purposely made sure that I would feel some pain as well.

I ran to the bathroom with my one visible eye to see if I could stop the pain in some way. As I glanced at myself in the mirror, my left eye being protected by my two hands, I quickly removed my hands the way a mother does when she plays "Peek-a-Boo" with her little one.

Remember what I said about the "craftiness in the hands of an artist whose first love is abuse"? Up until now, Yanna had been pretty good at not leaving any visible marks. There was a deep red mark with little polka dots surrounding the outer corner of my eye and upper left corner of my chin. I cringed as I gently touched the swollen hill on my face. How could I face my family? How could I let my mom see me like this? She'd probably laugh, just like she did in the hospital when I tried to take my life, one of the several ways I used as a cry for help.

I thought of possible ways to conceal the redness I knew would shortly turn into a dark bluish black color. The only solution I could come up with was my mother's foundation. Although my mother's complexion was much more lighter than mine due to her Asian descent, her light-colored foundation was the only option I had. Before I could put on a few coats of makeup three shades lighter than my skin tone, I needed to put some ice on my eye to control the swelling. That barbarian still hadn't come into the room to see if I was all right! He was just worried about his knuckles. Sorry punk! But if he was a punk, what did that make me?

Scene II: Betrayed With a Kiss

I thought about how stupid I was. He could have really messed my eye up. My eyes were already sensitive, and when I was younger, I experienced the shock of having a piece of metal fly into one of my eyes. I remember when it first happened. I thought I was blind, but I couldn't see because I had my eye shut so tightly. There was not a hint of light coming through although I was outside on a bright and sunny day. All I could see was darkness and large ovals of indescribable colors floating around in front of my eyelids.

I ran past Yanna, who was now sitting on the couch pretending he didn't know what he had just done. While I was making my ice pack, I saw Yanna in the corner of my good eye get up and go into the bedroom. Anger continued to fill my heart as the blood raced through my veins, running its cycle of grabbing the oxygen it needed from my lungs. It then continued through the rest of my body, supplying it with the necessary amount oxygen it needed.

I could feel my heart pounding. I looked down to see if it was pounding through my chest. I took my right hand that wasn't holding the sandwich bag of ice cubes and placed it on my chest. I could feel the hard labor of my heart as I tried to soothe it with the caressing of my hand. As I continued to stare at the circular motion my hand was making, saline-filled drops fell from my eyes, landing on my busy hand. Both of my hands started to shake while my blood continued to race throughout every blood vessel.

The anger started to intensify, making the thought of revenge seem sweet. Scenes of every sick man started flashing before my eyes. He was evil, and he deserved to die. I scanned the room, with my left eye profusely blinking, causing the room to look like it had a disco light, searching for a sharp object like the one I found underneath the mattress in that small four-room apartment.

"Boo, come here!" I heard Yanna calling for me. Wait a minute; I needed some more time. I don't have a weapon and I need a plan. If I do this, I can't turn back. I need to go through with this. I played the scene in my head. If I stabbed him with a knife and missed, or if I didn't do it hard enough to take him out, he'd probably take it from me and make me the victim.

"Boo!" This time there was more sharpness in the tone of his voice. He didn't hold the double "oo" long enough to make it sound as if he was singing the nickname he had for me and probably used for his other women.

"Wait a minute. I'm getting some ice," I replied in a somewhat confident voice but not so overbearing to cause him to get up and want to "straighten" me out. I walked toward the darkened basement bedroom, both hands placed behind my back.

"I don't have a plan, oh God, what am I going to do? God, help me. Tell me what to do." My hands began sweating under the metal handles of my mother's sewing scissors. I remembered when I dropped them on my toe and blood started seeping out of my white tights. These scissors will be sharp enough. I just have to remember to hold them tightly and not let go.

"Oh God help me. What am I doing?" As the room got closer and closer, my heart pounded more and more. I knew it had to be jumping out of my chest now. Yanna was sitting on the corner of the bed, gesturing me to come close to him. He quickly glanced at my bruised eye, then immediately focused on another area of my face. Did he feel a little guilty? No, I don't think so.

He was probably thinking, "See what you made me do?" They all do that. "They" meaning the people sickened by this disease of abusing others. They will abuse you physically and tell you that you made them do it. They will emotionally and mentally abuse you, telling you what they have to put up with. They will tell you that you are a nobody; that no one else will put up with your mess; that no one cares about you or wants you; and that no one will help you. And all physical abuse leads into mental and emotional abuse. You will be emotionally scarred by physical abuse. The two usually go hand in hand.

This disease by means of contact (physical abuse) and/or airborne (verbal abuse) then infects us. We can also get infected by witnessing the people we love who have endured this sort of abuse as well. The end results are the battered becoming co-dependents. We end up staying with the abusers because we either believe what they are saying about us to be true or feel that we are the only ones who understand them and could help them with their problems. Some believe the lie that they will never hit us again. In a way, and I'm just speaking for myself, I felt responsible. Am I alone in this?

As Yanna concentrated on another area of my face with his legs cocked open, he reached his arms out and pulled me closer to him; luckily he grabbed my hips. I quickly moved my arms from behind my back and wrapped them around him, careful not to let him see the sharp object.

"Did you see what you did to my eye?" Now I asked not as a question but more like a statement with anger in my voice. I didn't want any answers. I was sick of all the apologies and justifications. I heard them one too many times. Each and every sorry word that came out of his mouth fell on deaf ears. I continued to contemplate his fate now in my hands as my body stiffened. I felt the blood flow through my brain, giving me a rush I had never felt before. I felt flushed. I felt hunger and a thirst to feel his blood on my hands.

This disease I had now contracted made me want to cause pain. It made me desire the power to have my enemies cower, asking me for mercy with their cries and pleas, while begging me to stop. The more this sickening infestation manifested in my heart, the tighter I gripped the shears. The wetness had already evaporated. I had full control of the dagger and was ready to leap upon my enemy like a lion does a gazelle; to devour him, like a python does a mouse. I positioned the blades on the tip of his spinal cord waiting for that moment with each of his empty and hollow words feeding this desire more and more. Suddenly I felt something holding me back. I started thinking about my son and what would become of him. Then I began thinking of this man, sick with a disease for which he would be in constant denial.

"Do it! Do it! Remember the broken slab of wood from the couch he threw you against? Remember him throwing you against the wall? Think about Jerah. Who will take care of your son? Will you ever forgive yourself? Think about the blood running from your nose! Now you have a black eye! He will find the scissors and kill you with them! Do it! Do it now! This is your last chance!" These thoughts continued to race in my mind.

I tightened my grip once again. I felt the stiffness in his back. His body was rigid. His mind was uncertain of what cold object pressed against his spine. I increased the pressure of the blade, causing it to dig deeper and deeper, but not quite, inside his flesh. We looked deep into each other's eyes. There was a moment of silence that seemed to last a lifetime. This would be the last time he would ever look into my eyes. "This will be the last time you ever touch me again. Get out of my house right now or I will kill you," I commanded him.

Tears fell from my eyes as I sat there shaking, while staring at that shiny, long, and sharp dagger. I still managed to keep the tight grip on the handle, which now left my fingers stiff, like an action figure's hand, shaped to hold a sword. I won this battle! I took back the power that I had given him! I did not understand or appreciate the magnitude of that priceless word, power. When you do not know the value of something that you possess, you may neglect it or sometimes freely give it away. You fail to realize you have given away your rights, the privileges we have inherited as a child of God, through the death of Jesus Christ.

> *The Spirit Himself [thus] testifies together with our own spirit, [assuring us] that we are children of God. And if we are [His] children, then we are [His] heirs also: heirs of God and fellow heirs with Christ [sharing His inheritance with Him]; only we must share His suffering if we are to share His glory.*
> (Romans 8:16-17, AMP)

We all have the power of choice. Unfortunately, so many of us take that power for granted. Many of us may make choices with an "eeny meany miney moe" mentality. My choices, however, stemmed from the lack of knowledge of who I was and the importance of my life. I did not know how valuable my life was. My master, at that time, was the prince of darkness. He had a plan to keep me from receiving what I had searched for. The enemy did not want me to find the truth about God. He did not want me to know that what I was searching for was in God and that God is LOVE. Little did the enemy know that all his plans were essential to bringing me closer to the one thing I had desired, which was love. Nor did he know that I would no longer be under his authority because I was chosen by the one and only God. The trials and tribulations were used to strengthen me for the battle, the battle that God says we have already won because the battle belongs to the Lord and He cannot lose!

With God's grace I survived that battle, yet I was still left wounded and bitter. Due to bitterness, I was determined to never allow anyone to physically abuse me again. I would defend myself before that would ever happen. Because I walked in fear, the enemy was still in control. I still allowed him to have power over me because I believed in his lies. I continued to believe I was unworthy of a healthy and fulfilling love. I would have to work to get what little I could grab on to and continue to do those same things to keep it.

> *The thief does not come except to steal, and to kill, and to destroy. I have come that they may have life, and that they may have it more abundantly.*
>
> (John 10:10, NKJV)

THE SECOND JUDAS

His name was Yovar. He was around twenty years old, very quiet, and on this night, very drunk. One of my favorite songs came on. It was one of those fast "dirty dancing" beats, so I decided to ask him to dance with me. I was a very good dancer, but Yovar on the other hand was really off beat. I tried my hardest to follow his creative off-beat moves, but it was impossible! I blamed it on the alcohol and politely told him that we must be a little too drunk to dance. This may sound as if I think I was all that, but to be honest with you, when it came to dancing I really was. Anytime I was on the dance floor everyone watched, including the envious girls, but they would always join in. The men would sit back and wait their turn, never to get it, because I was usually dating someone.

Yovar and I returned to the table to get more acquainted. I asked him about his family. I asked if there was a history of twins in his family because I always had a desire to have twins and heard having twins was hereditary.

He told me his mother and aunt were twins and that his uncle just had twins. He has more potential than I thought! Not only was he smart, but he also had an additional quality that only one other person I knew possessed. And God knows how much I wanted twins, two girls to be exact. I asked him if he would use my phone number if I gave it to him. He misunderstood me by thinking I said lose it and told me no. I looked at him as if he was crazy. "You're not going to use my number if I give it to you?" I asked. I never had anyone turn me down before, so I was a little shocked. "Yes, yes, I'll use it. I thought you asked would I lose it." We had a good laugh about the misunderstanding, and I actually started feeling a little more comfortable with him. I was concerned that he was a little strange since he hardly talked and seemed very standoffish. He surprised me that he had the ability to laugh. I felt I had done my job at making him feel comfortable and that I in turn felt comfortable.

After a few weeks we started dating. Yovar was very intelligent and had a lot of musical talent. He played the clarinet, some kind of African drums, and a little of the sax. He told me his last girlfriend, while a teenager, died of leukemia. I found that her death devastated Yovar more than I had imagined. I told Yovar when I graduated from college I planned on moving to Delaware. I felt there would be more opportunities for me in Delaware. I also believed there would be a better chance of getting to know my father more. Unfortunately, my father and I had not gotten any closer; in fact, I felt further away from him than I did when I was in Kansas. However, I believed the Lord would build a strong relationship between the both of us.

I told Yovar that if he wanted to be with me, he had to come with me to Delaware. He wanted to be with me, but he still had time left to serve in the military. His platoon was given orders to go oversees for some type of drill or training. Well, Yovar and I both did not want him to go.

The men in his platoon questioned whether Yovar was mentally stable enough to go. There were also a few of the guys in his platoon wondering if it would be a good idea for Yovar to go. Yovar was very quiet and hardly communicated with anyone in his platoon, and they were concerned for everyone's safety.

Scene II: Betrayed With a Kiss

A few of the higher-ranked guys called me in to have a special meeting to discuss Yovar's condition. They informed me that Yovar was getting psychological testing done while they asked me questions about how Yovar interacted with me. I told them that he talked to me all the time, but there were times when he would get real quiet.

They asked me if I thought he should go with them overseas, which gave me the opportunity to make it sound like a bad idea. In a few weeks to a month, they gave Yovar an honorable discharge from the military. Later I would find that the decision was based on the results they received from his psychological testing. They diagnosed Yovar with personality disorder.

I desperately wanted twins, and Yovar knew this. However, I wondered if God was ever going to let me have children again because of the abortion I had gotten. But God showed Himself to be merciful while I was still a slave to sin.

But thanks be to God that, though you used to be slaves to sin, you wholeheartedly obeyed the form of teaching to which you were entrusted.

(Romans 6:17, NIV)

Since Yovar and I planned on getting married and buying a house when we went to Delaware I did not see anything wrong with getting pregnant.

As I sat back, I remembered all the events that took place in that house. There were a few precious and priceless memories along with some dark and heavy ones. I was unable to erase a particular memory from my mind.

I recalled the coolness of the ceramic tile as I walked bare foot on the kitchen floor. I could feel the cool breeze playing in each strand of my hair as I leaned on the ledge of that large high-rise deck, forgetting the fact that I was afraid of heights. We painted the deck a brick red, which clearly did not match the color of the house.

The master bedroom had its own large private bathroom. The toilet was separated from the bathtub although, within the same area. I remember the anger I felt when I found that the flooring was not completed. I looked down at my feet to see the unevenness of the floor, although the closing papers were already signed.

I watched Alisa peacefully sleeping in her beautiful round Liberty Crib dressed in pure white linen. She had straight, thick, jet-black hair that completely covered her sweet-smelling head. I remember the first steps Alisa took on her very first birthday. She and her brother shared together as we celebrated his eleventh year of living. Alisa and Jerah were ten years and six days apart.

Everyone would tell me that I did not look old enough to have an eleven-year-old. I would politely respond by telling them, "I'm not." I was fifteen years old when I had Jerah, but thank God He got me through. He was the only one who made it possible, the only ONE who kept my sanity although many times I felt as if my world was falling apart.

How could a fifteen-year-old possibly raise a young boy to become a man, a young man who would truly love the Lord and seek Him with all of his heart? How could I raise a young man who would fish for other men like himself? A young man who would come to know the true love that God has for His children regardless of social status, race, or lack of having a positive male role figure in his life?

How could a single mother of two build a house on solid ground through a violent storm? I have but one answer, and His name is Jesus. Jesus held me at the times when I could no longer stand. I was being carried by His grace and mercy along the water as I held my children. Jesus helped me reach the shore. The violent ocean waters tried to engulf me. I was left with remnants of what the Lord would not allow to be destroyed. These are the pieces of my life that God is putting back together as He continues to mold and make me.

I knew in the depths of my spirit that the house was never meant to be mine, but I did not want to accept that thought. I felt I had no other choice but to remain in the relationship. If I wanted my daughter to be raised by both of her parents, then I would have to stay with her father even if it meant giving up my happiness. However, when the safety of my children were in jeopardy, that was when I had to draw the line.

I told God that I did not make enough money and I didn't even own that house. How could I raise two children by making seven dollars an hour with no place to live? So in desperation, I prayed for God's will. "God, please, if this relationship is not Your will, then end it, but make a way for me and my children. Oh dear God, please make a way." Shortly after, my children and I experienced the results of that answered prayer.

Jerah introduced me to his new friend's mother. She was a wonderful, loving, compassionate, and very gifted woman. She and her husband welcomed our family over for dinner one night. It was very peaceful there, a feeling I had not felt for some time. When the relationship between Yovar and I began to get rough, she opened up her house to the kids and me.

One morning in January of the year 1999, God held my kids and me tightly in His arms as He carried us through a violent storm. As with the situation with Yanna and me, Yovar and I only had one means of transportation, which was my car.

I would drive to work every morning with Alisa and Yovar in the car so he could take the car. He would drop Alisa off later that day at the babysitter's and then drive himself to work. After I would get off from work, I would take two buses that would eventually lead me to the front of a housing development that I would have to walk completely through in order to get to Yovar's job. It would take an hour and a half to finally get home, but it saved us money that we didn't have much of.

This morning was not like any other morning. We had hardly spoken with one another since our breakup. He had decided about a week ago, after living in the basement for weeks without speaking with me, that he no longer wanted to remain in the relationship and that he only wanted to be friends.

He had this wild notion that we should continue to live together as roommates. This way, Alisa would be raised by both of her parents under the same roof. He also believed we could both live our own separate lives by dating other people while still living together.

I looked at him as if he was out of his mind! I actually responded with a few words to let him know just how crazy he was and how crazy he must have thought I was to agree with something like that. Who in their right mind would allow a man they were once engaged to, to sleep with another woman under the same roof? I know this fool must have been on some kind of drugs! However, I knew he did not take drugs, smoke, or drink. That was just his way of thinking! Talk about scary.

Alisa just turned one, and we lived in the house less than a year and then he decides to drop the bomb. I let him know that if he ever let another woman that he was dating come into our home, and then on top of that sleep with her, neither one of them would be leaving the house in one piece! Now I wasn't saved at the time, but are there some saved people in the house who honestly wouldn't have wanted to knock a little bit of sense in him? Can I please get a witness?

We were driving down the highway while I was trying to place a guilt trip on him, by letting him know how hurt I was.

"You know, Yovar, you just can't come into someone's life, agree to have a child together with plans of getting married, and then one day decide you just want to be friends. You can't play with people's lives like that and think that it's not going to come back to you. What makes you think you could just come into my life and treat me like that? You wasted my time. You are selfish. You are only thinking about yourself! You don't even care about the kids and me. What are we going to do? I can't afford a place of my own, and I don't want to lose Alisa."

"You don't have to move. No one said you had to move," he replied. "You could live in the house and we could raise Alisa together. You're the one who keeps saying you have to go," he answered in an abrupt and heartless manner.

"I'm not going to live with you while you're dating other people. It wouldn't bother you just a little to see me with another man, let alone

Scene II: Betrayed With a Kiss

sleeping with him in the same house?" I asked with a puzzled look on my face.

"No, it wouldn't bother me if we agreed we were only friends," he answered with a nonchalant look on his face. The one he always has; detached and dispassionate. "I don't want to talk about it anymore!" he said in a cold manner.

As we continued the ride to my job, I persistently tried to get him to understand the betrayal I felt while he relentlessly showed no remorse or regret. My eyes were full of tears when we finally reached the entrance to my job. I looked over at Yovar and could see that he was frustrated, but he refused to look at me. He just stared into space. I knew how Yovar got when he was frustrated. Like many people when frustrated, he did not like to be bothered, but unlike many he would separate himself from the world. It was as if his mind would travel off to this faraway place that no one could reach.

I could remember him explaining to me how he would "contemplate." Contemplating was his religion's way of praying. Contemplation, he explained, was how you, or in this case he and they involved in the same religion, would have their spirit leave the body and join God in order to have this closeness or oneness with God. He would repeat this word over and over that meant love in his religion. I actually tried it a few times, but it would never work for me. I did not understand then what I was getting myself involved with. I just thank God that He knew and protected me from this demonic practice.

Let me tell you something right now, and if it's one of the few things you remember from reading any of this, I pray right now that you never forget this. Read this statement ten times if need be and engrave it on your heart. Do not under any circumstances believe and allow anyone to lead you to believe that you need to sing, chant, hum any word or series of words in order to have a relationship with or let alone call on God. All you have to do is speak His name one time. God is always ready for us to speak to Him. God is omnipresent, He is everywhere at all times.

Where can I go from your Spirit? Where can I flee from your presence? If I go up to the heavens, you are there; if I make

> my bed in the depths, you are there. If I rise on the wings of the dawn, if I settle on the far side of the sea, even there your hand will guide me, your right hand will hold me fast. If I say, "Surely the darkness will hide me and the light become night around me," even the darkness will not be dark to you; the night will shine like the day, for the darkness is as light to you.
> (Psalm 139:7-12, NIV)

After you have called on God, simply tell Him that you are ready to have a relationship with Him. He is already there waiting.

> For it is with your heart that you believe and are justified, and it is with your mouth that you confess and are saved. As the Scripture says, "Anyone who trusts in him will never be put to shame." For there is no difference between Jew and Gentile—the same Lord is Lord of all and richly blesses all who call on him, for, "Everyone who calls on the name of the Lord will be saved."
> (Romans 10:10-13, NIV)

I was sitting there looking at his face that wore this emptiness, trying to understand, trying to comprehend how after two years and a baby, he was able to completely turn off his feelings. I turned my head to look at Alisa sleeping in her car seat—peaceful, unaware of the fate that lay ahead. Seeing her sleeping reminded me of the way Yovar would put her to sleep.

He worked the evening shift (3:00 p.m. to 11:30 p.m.) and would watch Alisa during the day while I worked. The only problem is that he would be very tired. After he fed Alisa in the morning he would go to sleep and make Alisa go to sleep with him whether she wanted to or not. He had this method of putting her to sleep that I was very uncomfortable with. He would lay her next to him, and in order to keep the sunlight out of her eyes, he would cover her eyes with his hands until she would eventually fall asleep. She would move her head side-to-side trying to escape his hand, but he would follow her eyes with his hand until his goal was met.

Scene II: Betrayed With a Kiss

I constantly begged him to take Alisa to the babysitter's earlier or all day if he needed so he could get some rest. I tried to explain to him over and over that he could not simply feed her and then make her sleep all day without spending any quality time with her by playing, reading, and talking to her. But he refused to listen to me and continued to care for her in the same manner day after day. I would be so frightened at work that I would call constantly just to make sure everything was OK, reminding him that he needed to do some constructive things with Alisa.

Once he left Alisa and Jerah at home alone one night to pick me up from work. He picked me up an hour and a half late with no children in the car, and we lived approximately twenty minutes away. Jerah was about ten years old and Alisa was almost a year old. Jerah was not old enough to be left with Alisa, and on top of that he was a heavy sleeper. If there were ever a fire in that house, he may not wake up in time. All types of horrifying thoughts replayed themselves in my head on the way home that night. The way they were as I watched my sweet baby sleep.

I couldn't go to work in that emotional shape, nor did I feel comfortable with leaving her with him. "I can't work today. I'm not working." I quickly explained as I took the keys out of the ignition. I ran into the building, hopped in the elevator, and ran into my department's office so I could ask my supervisor if he would give me an emergency day.

My eyes were bloodshot red from crying, and I could hardly breathe. I spoke with my supervisor and the secretary, explaining briefly what was going on and that I couldn't work that day. I asked the supervisor to escort me back to my car just in case Yovar decided to "act up."

Once we got out of the elevator that led back to the lobby I saw Yovar sitting on one of the lobby couches holding Alisa. I looked at Ufara my supervisor. "That's him with the baby," I whispered as we slowly approached Yovar, unaware of his intentions.

"What are you doing?" Yovar asked in a stern and hardhearted manner. "We're going home," I quickly answered. I was not in the mood to get into a confrontation in front of my supervisor and the guy who was sitting behind the information desk. We all walked to the car. Yovar got in the car and started putting Alisa into her car seat while I was talking to Ufara. My supervisor asked me if I would be all right. I told him I would not be all right thinking about what would happen once we got home.

Ufara walked back into the hospital and began speaking with Zephi behind the information desk. Yovar continued to ask me what I was doing. At that time I simply replied, "Don't worry about it. We're just going home."

"What do you think you're doing, Lorna?" he asked again, but this time with irritation in his voice. Before I could answer him, he quickly reached for the car keys, commanding me to give him the keys. He lounged after me as I swiftly took the keys and jumped out of the car. I don't remember whether or not I had closed my door or if Yovar had. I just remember motioning to Ufara for help, who by the grace of God was still in the lobby talking to Zephi.

Ufara rushed back outside to see what had happened. While I was explaining to him what had just occurred, Yovar locked all the car doors. Ufara and I looked at the car once we heard the locks click and then at each other. "He just locked the doors," Ufara stated with deep concern. "I don't know why; I still have the keys," I answered.

At that point I asked Ufara to call security and have Yovar removed from my car. In what seemed less than sixty seconds, four or five security guards were rushing toward my car. I could not believe my eyes! It was like an army of soldiers coming to my defense, ready to charge my enemy!

One of the security guards knocked on the passenger window where Yovar was sitting, asking Yovar to unlock the door. Another guard started to ask me questions. I watched Yovar as he tried to ignore the officer at the window. At one point Ufara had asked me if Yovar was on drugs because when Yovar was sitting in the lobby with Alisa, he was acting like someone who could be on drugs. I told Ufara no; that he didn't even smoke or drink (any more).

Scene II: Betrayed With a Kiss

Yovar and the security guard were exchanging words since Yovar refused to get out of the car. The officer tried to explain to Yovar that he needed to get out of the car since I was the owner and wanted him removed. Yovar kept arguing with the officer about taking Alisa out as well. I prayed that he would not be able to take Alisa, and again, God answered my prayer. Yovar was escorted out of my car and I then drove off with Alisa.

Ufara told me to call him to discuss the possibility of me taking a few days off in case I needed to take care of whatever business I felt necessary. I just thanked him and all the security officers for all of their help as I rode off.

Just as in the past, I raced home to get my things out. Where was I going from there? I didn't know and I didn't care. Oh Lord, why does it feel like I was here before? Was there not in the past another bright, sunny, weekday morning that involved me trying to escape a mad man? Hmm. I found myself in another unhealthy relationship, going through the same cycle.

On the way home I kept praying to God, asking Him to help me, asking Him, "Where can I go?" The first name that came to my heart was Bryanna. I'll go over there. I have nowhere else to go, and just a few weeks ago she told me if anything happens and if I needed her, that I know where to find her. "Oh God I can't go over her house. It will be the three of us and her whole family in the same house. I can't do that. She and her husband won't let us stay there." The more I kept reasoning with God, the less it was working. I found myself in front of her driveway.

I took Alisa out of her car seat and rang their doorbell. Her husband answered, and I quickly started pleading with him to take Alisa. "I have to get out of the house. Can we please stay with you?" I earnestly asked him. "Where's Bryanna?" I continued." Her husband immediately asked me to calm down and to slowly explain to him what was going on. I explained to him what had taken place a little slower but not any calmer. During the explanation Bryanna finally came to the door to get in on all the drama. She calmly told me that the kids and I could stay and to quickly get the things we needed and come back over. She told me they would watch Alisa until I came back.

My head was heavy, my eyes were burning and red, and my stomach felt like I was having one of my premenstrual episodes. I drove up to the house, five town houses away and about fifteen steps from Bryanna's front door. I parked the car in the driveway and quickly ran for the door. I unlocked the front door and looked at the deadbolt, remembering that I did not have the key for it. I would have to remove the deadbolt so that I could get back into the house if I needed to, but I would do that later.

I ran upstairs and started packing all the kids' clothes I could place in bags. I quickly packed through all the tears and crying out to God, asking Him why this was happening and what was I going to do. I thought I would put most of the things in the trunk of my car so that I could get more, but I had to move fast. I did not want to be greeted at the door by Yovar on one of my trips to the car. It had seemed too much like deja vu. "God, please don't let him come before I get back to Bryanna's house, please, God, please," I pleaded.

I took all of Alisa's diapers and baby food she needed. I grabbed all the toothbrushes and toothpaste and both of the kids' shoes. I looked around in our bedroom where we once smiled and laughed, although the tears and cries outweighed the joy. I looked at my television, VCR, and stereo system and knew I had to leave them. They were the least of my concerns, but I knew that he would probably destroy everything I had. Eventually he did.

A few weeks later I would find my television and VCR outside in pieces. He destroyed my telephone. Kicked my stereo system through the back of the armoire that it sat in. He took the one mirror that was on my dresser and destroyed that too. All that remained were tiny pieces of glass on our bedroom floor. The things I worked so hard to get and maintain, he had destroyed. He also tried to destroy my life, but he failed.

What the enemy does to destroy us, God will use to build us up and make us stronger than we ever were. Thank you, Judas; you were the best traitor of them all! But I have learned it was because you were the most hurt of them all. When you have darkness (bitterness, resentment, and unforgiveness) in your heart, it becomes the enemy's playground. Satan is the prince of darkness.

Scene II: Betrayed With a Kiss

We'll believe his lies and behave accordingly to what we believe in. What a man believes or thinks is from his heart.

Yovar was bitter about the loss of his last girlfriend, who died of leukemia at a young age. Yovar still had not let go of her. He was not healed from her death, and I am not sure that he is to this day.

While I was frantically packing, something told me to grab those notebooks that Yovar wrote in. He would write these "Initiatives Reports" for the "religion" he was practicing. He also had another journal that his mother had given him during her last visit around Alisa and Jerah's birthday. I was so interested in knowing what he was thinking since he didn't really speak to me about his feelings, well at least not during the last few months.

When I had finished packing all that I could without spending too much time in that house so I would not get caught, I took one last look at the house, never knowing if the kids and I would ever live there again.

If you are reading this, Yovar, know that God will take away your pain. He will heal you from your loss and restore all that was taken from you. Your first step is to ask for forgiveness. Are you angry with God? Do you feel He took her away from you? Only you can answer that question. I don't know what's in your heart, and you may not realize that there may be some truth to that question, "Are you angry at God because you feel He has taken her away from you?" Second, after you have asked for forgiveness of the bitterness that has been embedded so deep within your heart, let it go. Allow God to heal you. Not a God that speaks through the light, but the ONE and ONLY God that speaks to your heart. God is the light. Seek Him with all your heart.

The Bible is God's Word. Every if, and, or, and but came from God. You cannot believe just some of the things that are in the Bible; you have to believe them all. If you don't believe all of it, then you don't believe in God, plain and simple.

In the beginning was the Word, and the Word was with God, and the Word was God.

(John 1:1, NIV)

It's all the truth, and God is Truth; nothing in Him is a lie. God is a God that cannot and will not lie, ever, regardless of any situation or circumstance. Remember when you asked me, "How do you know that the Bible is all true, and that the other books other religions believe in are not true?" I told you then and I am telling you now—I know it in my spirit without a doubt that every word in the Bible is from God and that all of it is true. If anything does not line up with the Bible, then it is not of God. Man alone made it up.

Bryanna was like an angel in disguise. She was so gracious in her giving not only to me, but most importantly toward my children. She taught me so many things and helped me be strong through the whole ordeal. She encouraged me to go and press charges against Yovar and file to have a "Protection From Abuse" order not only for me but for the children as well, especially Alisa.

She took me to the police department and the family courthouse. All the legal terms were so foreign to me. Once I went to the courthouse I had to fill out documentation explaining why I needed the Protection From Abuse (PFA) order against Yovar. They would determine by the statement I had given the severity of the abuse. That in return would affect the promptness of getting a PFA order. After a phone call or two and a hearing in front of a commissioner, I was issued an emergency PFA that very same day. I was told that I would soon be getting a court order to appear in court, for a hearing, by mail. The fact that Yovar demonstrated signs of abuse toward Alisa in particular gave the court reason to order the emergency PFA.

I told them about the hole Yovar punched in the wall above Alisa's changing table because he was running late for work one day. She had a bowel movement, so he had to change her. I also explained the incident of when he covered Alisa's mouth. He was changing her diaper and she was crying because she had a terrible diaper rash. To keep her from crying he covered her mouth. While he was covering her mouth he was also covering her nose; this caused her to almost suffocate. I remember running up the stairs because her screams had changed into muffled sounds. He had covered her mouth and her nose to where she could not breathe.

I do not remember if I added the time when he elbowed me while I was driving with the kids in the car because I didn't feel like giving him his ATM card right away. Every time he was frustrated he reacted in a violent manner.

One day I couldn't take it any longer. We were engaged and planned on having the pastor marry us. I suggested that we go see him together in person to ask him to do us the honor of uniting us before God. Well, for some reason Yovar felt it wasn't necessary for us to go in person to ask the pastor. He felt we could just ask him over the phone. At the time I did not see why he did not want to speak with the pastor in person. I am the type of person that would rather discuss or present something face-to-face with the person involved. But further on through our argument I came to find the true reason why he didn't want to ask the pastor personally.

I was getting ready for church that morning while we were having this argument about speaking with the pastor. I was ironing my clothes and arguing with Yovar at the same time while he was obviously not getting ready. How could he get ready if he's too busy arguing with me?

Well, he got so frustrated that he yelled at me to shut up. At the same time, he took his index finger, placed it on my shoulder, and pushed me with it. At that point I was very upset, no, let's say pissed off, because this was not the first time Yovar had done this to me. Telling me to shut up, that's all good, no problem, I could take that. I'm not saying I would shut up. However, to push or touch me in a negative way, I would not tolerate. He pushed me the same way as I was walking down the steps when I was pregnant while having an argument at my father's house. But this particular day, I decided that it would be the last time.

"What's your problem? You can't keep your fingers off of me?" I yelled at him with my eyes full of tears. There are two reasons why I cry. One, because I am sad, hurt, or depressed. The other reason is because I am angry, so angry that my eyes start tearing up and most often, my hands would shake. In this case, the tears were from anger.

As I was asking Yovar what his problem was, he was shaking his head back and forth mocking every word I was saying. I continued ironing my clothes and exchanging words with him. I was getting angrier and angrier because he made the argument out to be a circus act.

"All right," I said, after he pushed me for the last time. "I'm getting sick of this! I'm tired of you pushing me! If you want to do something to me, do it now. If you have a problem with me, then we need to settle it now. If you want to fight me, then let's get it over with!"

I was standing there with tears in my eyes. My hands were shaking while I was trying to iron my skirt. I couldn't get my pantyhose off fast enough, and Yovar was still shaking his big head back and forth, with his two big protruding ears that were now as red as his face while he was continuing to mock me.

He had no sympathy. He didn't care that he just laid his hands on me after I told him one too many times not to do it again. Yovar knew that I had been in a physically abusive relationship and that I was not going to allow anyone to put his or her hands on me. He should have remembered the first time he slapped me soon after I had the baby.

We were at my dad's house in the bedroom beside my dad's while my dad was in his room watching TV. Yovar was being rough with the baby when he was changing her diaper because he was tired. Was it my fault that she needed her diaper changed late at night? Well, like any other time he got frustrated because he was tired, and I asked him to change her diaper. He was fastening the strap on her diaper but putting a little bit too much pressure on her navel where the umbilical cord was still attached. So I told him not to be so rough with her.

Why did I even open my mouth? He got more frustrated and a little rougher with her. So I in return got more upset and start yelling at him to be careful or he'd hurt her. OK, now the both of us were yelling at one another until Yovar decides to take it one step further. Out of nowhere Yovar slaps me in the face, adding the statement, "That's what you deserve." I think there was silence for about a millisecond, just enough time for me to realize that this man must have totally lost his mind! That was all she wrote! The next thing I knew, I was laying with my back on the bed, legs dangling off the bed with

Scene II: Betrayed With a Kiss

Yovar over me yelling in my face. All I could think about at the moment was not letting him hit me again.

As he was trying to get closer and closer to my face, I had my left hand around his neck with my nails dug deep into his flesh. This didn't stop him from trying to shut me up with his screams while his face was getting closer and closer to my face until our foreheads almost touched. The closer he got, the deeper my grip became. I was determined to stop him from hitting me again, even if it meant separating his head from his neck with my five claws. I was terrified. He had never been directly physical with me. He just threw a few things. But to top it off, while my dad was in the next room! I don't know what caused him to get off me, but once he did, I quickly got up and went into my father's room.

I was explained to my dad what happened, and then he had a little discussion with Yovar. My dad was not really interested in what Yovar had to say. Dad just wanted to get his point across. I was sitting by my dad on the bed watching for the first time my father protecting me.

He looked Yovar dead in his eyes as he firmly stated these words: "Look`, man, I have never hit Lorna before, and I'm her daddy, so don't you ever hit her again. You understand?" Now my dad may not have said these words in the same order, but he did say them. This was the first time I ever felt safe by my dad's side.

After I took my pantyhose off, I ran out of the room and told Jerah to get dressed and go outside for a few minutes. I did not want him to see Yovar and me fight, although he did hear us on several occasions. While I was rushing Jerah to go outside so Yovar could get whatever he had on his shoulders off, Jerah was crying and pleading with us not to fight. "No, Mommy, I don't want you guys to fight!" Jerah pleaded. "No, I'm tired of this. I'm tired of him putting his hands on me!" I explained.

I went back into the bedroom and found that Yovar wasn't there. I slammed the door shut and locked it while I was inside. Yovar came back and tried to open the door. He frantically shook the door while yelling and hollering a few words at me. For a few seconds there was a moment of silence, and then the door flew open. Yovar kicked the door opened and the siding had pulled away from the wall. I jumped at the sight but still tried to maintain that "I'm not scared of you" composure. I can't remember what happened soon after that, but we both finally made our way downstairs, and Jerah was out on the deck crying as Yovar and I were face-to-face.

"Go ahead and fight me if that's what you want to do! You'd better get it over now, because I am sick and tired of you putting your hands on me!" I screamed while tears quickly raced down my cheeks. Yovar got down on his knees and held my legs tightly, like a child at their first day of school begging its mother not to leave him or her.

My body shook. I just wanted it to be over. I just wanted us to be a happy family. I wanted Alisa and Jerah to be raised by two loving parents. I did not want to leave out the "loving" part. I wanted the fighting to end, the yelling to stop, and the physical and mental abuse to end. I was tired. I was so sick and tired of being sick and tired.

"Oh God, help me. Please take this pain away." I cried out to Him right before I left the house after packing. God did, in His own way, in His perfect timing, and He held me tightly the whole way through.

It took the authorities about two weeks to serve Yovar with the PFA (Protection From Abuse) papers. The family court granted the kids and me the house and child support for Alisa. Yovar could not come in contact with my children or myself (meaning he would have to leave the house). This included no contact through phone, mail, or through a third party. Yovar violated almost every condition of the order.

After Bryanna and I found out that Yovar was served the PFA order, we called the authorities and had him removed. Yovar was incarcerated and remained in prison for a few weeks.

While in jail, through his stubbornness, he decided to again violate the order by writing me a letter, although it was addressed to Bryanna. In his letter he was apologizing and asking me to take him back. I knew that if I took him back, it would be like trying to commit suicide; at least that's how my son put it (and I agreed). There was no way I would go back to a life full of verbal and mental abuse, which sometimes led to physical abuse as well.

I wept every night and sometimes throughout the day. I did not know what was going to happen with the children and me. Even though the court granted me the house, I had no idea how I would pay the mortgage. A six hundred and seventy-one dollar a month mortgage, day-care expenses with two children, on a seven dollar an hour job seemed impossible. The thought of it made my stomach burn. I knew I would not be able to move back into my father and stepmother's house. I also knew my family living near by would not help us, and the only one that would was eighteen hours away.

Although Bryanna made us feel welcomed, often I felt like we were imposing on her and her family. I could not have asked for a better friend than Bryanna. She was there for the children and me, like a mother with open arms who had not seen her child in years. Bryanna and the Lord both encouraged me and kept me strong.

THE UNFAITHFUL LOVER

My friend Tamir wanted to introduce me to one of his friends, Gideon. Gideon was his last name, which was the way we would address GIs (military personnel). I knew Tamir ever since the fifth grade, and now we were twenty-two years old and he was in the military. Since Fort Riley was basically a part of Junction City, the military had brought him back home.

Tamir planned for the six of us to go out to the club. This club was where a majority of the college students, including myself, would go out to. There was Tamir, his friends Jacob, Gideon, and another friend whose name I forget, along with Yedidah (Yedi) and myself.

As usual, I made sure that I was "good" ("good" was the term we used to indicate that we had drank enough alcohol and/or smoked enough weed) before we went to the club.

I was into smoking joints or blunts, although I preferred blunts since they held more weed. Yedi, on the other hand, was more into the alcohol. She took a couple of hits with me, but she made sure she was full of the liquor. When I smoked marijuana, I would achieve a high without the stomach or headaches. When the high started to die, I made sure that I would maintain it with the alcohol that we drank on the way to the "spot" of the night.

I remember my favorite drink, "Sex on the Beach." I thought I was "all that," but I was only a pawn for the enemy, but God is awesome. He would take my life and make a spectacle out of it in the devil's face.

After a night of drinking, smoking, and dancing we all decided to go to Jacob's. Jacob was married, but he and his wife were separated and, according to Jacob, planned on getting a divorce.

There was a song out by TLC called "Switch." If you don't like your partner or date, switch and take his friend. Well, in between all the drinking and smoking, the initial plans of me being hooked up with Gideon changed. Yedi was sitting with Gideon and Jacob had his eyes set on me. I was still interested in Gideon, but destiny had to happen and Gideon was not a part of my destiny. Jacob was married, separated, and supposed to be getting a divorce. Tamir, Gideon, and I were wondering how this switch ever happened. Tamir and Gideon thought I liked Jacob, and Gideon was not interested in Yedi.

Within weeks Jacob and I had gotten very close and begun dating. Like all the other relationships I was in, we quickly became intimate. Jacob was actually a very nice person whom I enjoyed spending my time with. I started spending so much time with him that I started neglecting my son again.

Jacob and I were both separated and spoke of divorcing our spouses. I was foolish to believe that he was actually going through a divorce with his wife. Why should I not believe him? I believed every other lie that was said to me, so why should this time be any different?

I wanted to believe that one of those men who told me they loved me truly meant it. I wanted the words they spoke to me to be truthful. But how could I recognize the truth when I myself was living a lie?

This was the second married man I was with, and both times I was still married, even though I knew I was getting a divorce. Even so, it did not negate the fact that I was guilty of committing adultery. Why would I continue allowing myself to be in a relationship with a married man? Years later I would come to learn that there was a generational curse of adultery and sexual immorality in my family. I had followed the footsteps of family members before me

David and I only remained married for financial reasons. We believed in our hearts too much had happened between the two of us to go back and start all over again.

He was in another relationship and had a baby while still being married to me. How could I go back? I myself had been in another relationship. So why would he want to come back? Although I knew I was getting a divorce, what made me think that the man I was with was really getting a divorce?

One of the men I was with told me he was getting a divorce while he was waiting on the birth of his twins. I was naïve to believe that he was actually going to divorce his wife although they were just beginning to start a family.

I remember when David found out about the affair. He approached him and his wife about it. His wife was terrified when David approached them in any other way but friendly. David was about 215 pounds and about 6 foot 2 inches. His wife begged David not to hurt her husband.

"He's a father now. Please don't hurt him." David only hurt him a little.

"I just jacked him up. I really didn't hurt him like I wanted to." Although David was able to release some of his frustration on the "other man" it still didn't take away the pain I caused by betraying him.

I found that David had also committed adultery with his sister's friend. This big, fat, ugly, football-looking chick I saw him dancing with at the club. I was so pissed off that I had to leave. She was too big to fight, and both of his sisters were there. His sisters never liked me and always accused me of cheating on David prior to our separation, even when I had no desire or thoughts of ever doing it.

I loved my husband very much. I cried often, wanting him to receive all the affection I had for him. David was never used to a woman being so affectionate toward him, and I was that type of woman. I felt rejected and empty inside. I cried suicide so many times that he just started ignoring my cries. I wanted David to fulfill the emptiness inside of me. I was trying to fill the void in me that only God Himself could fill.

Our relationship from day one was exhausting, but we had to prove everyone wrong. Everyone kept telling us not to get married. They warned us that marriage would change everything. We refused to believe their warnings. But when I think about it, our relationship was unhealthy to begin with. We were both very young. I was nineteen and David was about twenty years old.

He decided to join the army during my second year of college in order to better our lives. He did not believe he would do well in college. I tried to encourage him by telling him how smart he was and how much potential he had, but my words fell on deaf ears.

Living near a military base made the idea much more appealing. GI's seemed to have their lives together. They had a steady income, benefits, and the married couples lived in military housing, compliments of the government.

David's family was also military, along with mine. I was what you call a "military brat" but never really experienced military family living since my parents divorced while I was a young child. Nevertheless, my mother and I still had military benefits.

Jacob and I had been together for a few months now and getting very serious in our relationship. I basically lived there. I would go home every now and then just to get my clothes, sometimes Jerah, and to visit my dog, Scarface, a one-year-old Rottweiler.

One of the few days that I decided to stay home I invited my best friend over to get high with me. She knew that Jacob and I had been dating for quite some time now and how I felt about him. I wanted them to meet each other since they were the two most important people in my life at that time.

Once Jacob arrived, Hannah and I already had been smoking on a joint, so we were a little high, she more than me since she really did not smoke as often. Jacob and Hannah were getting along very well, which did not surprise me since they were both friendly people. After a while the three of us were all high.

I took Hannah in my bedroom and asked her to do something. I told her how much I cared about her and Jacob and how much I trusted the both of them. She wasn't too sure about doing it. I could tell that she was a little afraid and I was too. Between the high and me, she was convinced that it would be fun.

A few years later I finally got the opportunity to speak with Hannah again. She told me how much that day affected her. She was mentally and emotionally scarred from that situation that a so-called friend like me asked her to be involved in. The sick, perverted, sexual sin I committed in which I encouraged her to commit.

Months before that day I got Hannah involved in Jacob and me, a friend of mine had asked me to be involved in the same act. From that day on, I was bound by the spirit of bisexuality. Today would be another day I was reminded of that horrifying act.

I would relive the vision of Hannah's face and the pain I felt as I watched the wickedness of sexual immorality unfold before my very own eyes. I felt guilty for asking her to be involved in this malicious act. How I could ever take away her pain that I felt responsible for causing her? I now know the one man who could free her from her prison. His name is Jesus, and His blood was shed on the cross to cover all of our sins. The sins of yesterday, today, and tomorrow are forgiven by God. All we have to do is ask and believe.

I could see her face as she laid there while Jacob was having sex with her as I watched. I fondled her body in a way that only a man should be with a woman. I could tell that she did not want to be there. I believed she hoped that the weed was making her do it and perhaps for her it did. I, on the other hand, knew what I was involving her in. The highest high never made me do anything I did not want to do.

I knew a lot of people that would use alcohol and drugs as an excuse for their actions when most of them wanted to engage in those shameful acts. Why not blame it on the poisons? That would be the easy way out. As we took turns with Jacob, my feelings began to change. I suddenly felt fear, jealousy, and envy. But who was I jealous of? Was I jealous of Jacob being with her or with Hannah being with him?

I remember the attraction I felt toward her when I saw her laying in the bed with only in her panties and bra. Why was I feeling this way? I was so afraid of my feelings, but yet I wanted so badly to share them with her. But what would have become of our friendship? I didn't want to lose Hannah. She was one of my very best friends. For years I felt shame and guilt. I was so ashamed of thinking of Hannah in that way.

Hannah stuck with me through the battles in my marriage. She even cried with me one day on the couch while I pleaded with David to understand how I felt. Why didn't he understand? He was my husband. Did he not see that I was hurting inside? Did he not see that I was empty and needed him to give me what I needed to fill the void in my life? Why was he so cruel? What did he mean by saying, "You're not happy because you don't want to be happy"? I resented that remark. All I ever wanted was to be happy.

I had tried everything from sex, to alcohol, to drugs, to trying to be a good wife (from what I thought), to trying to be a good mother, a dedicated student, and a hard worker.

Scene II: Betrayed With a Kiss

Hannah left, and Jacob and I said our good-byes to her. I wondered whether he would leave me for her or she would stop being my friend. None of us ever spoke about that incident again. Not until years later was that event given life when Hannah told me how it affected her.

I wished I could have erased her pain, her memories, and every evil thought and tears she cried while trying to heal from this tragedy. But how do you erase a memory? What do you do when saying those two words I'm sorry with deepest sincerity has no meaning to the one who you have hurt? What is left when the one you love does not forgive you? Although they may decide not to forgive you, know that God will. If you asked God for forgiveness, you are free from the sins you committed. You should also forgive and love yourself. If God who is pure and holy forgives you, you also should forgive yourself because of the blood of Jesus that washes away our sins. We can live a life without shame and guilt of our pasts.

Therefore if any man be in Christ, he is a new creature: old things are passed away; behold, all things are become new.
                                        (2 Corinthians 5:17, KJV)

I am not sure when Jacob broke the news about his enlistment time being up and that he would be returning home, which was somewhere on the East Coast. Our relationship had gotten serious enough that we made plans for the two of us to get married. Jacob was to return home and eventually send for me. He would call at least every week to fill me in on the progress of settling in and getting things prepared for Jerah and me.

I heard from Jacob only once after he left. He was outside using a pay phone. It sounded like a car accident or some other serious incident in the background, which caused him to quickly get off the phone. He told me he would call me back later, but that was the last time that I ever heard his voice.

A few months later I found out that I was carrying his baby. I had no phone number to call him or address to write. And since he was no longer in the military, I couldn't even have him tracked down. I was twenty-two years old with a seven-year-old son and a child on the way. I had a decision to make. The decision I made would haunt me for several years.

My best friend John's sister and I had become very close. We both decided to be roommates beginning the next school semester, which would be in spring of 1995. Maxine was the only one besides John who knew that I had gotten pregnant again. I told John what I had planned to do, so he excused Maxine and me from work. Funny, John was my age and also my boss, but it was real cool having a best friend as a boss, at times.

Abortions were not as popular in my hometown as they were in other cities, so Maxine had to drive me to another city in order to get the procedure. I looked in the phone book for all the nearby clinics that performed this procedure. They suggested that I take a friend along because I may be too weak or in too much pain to drive myself back. That is probably the only reason why I told Maxine; otherwise it would have just been my little secret. You know, "just between God and me." Maxine had been at this clinic before; therefore she knew exactly how to get there.

As we approached the clinic we saw anti-abortionist picketing along the sidewalk toward the clinic. I remember one lady yelling, which actually sounded more like a cry. She was crying out, "You don't have to do this!" All I could think about was my situation. "You don't understand. This is the only option I have," I thought. I could never let my mom see me with another child. What made it worse was that I was still married and this child was not my husband's. We were separated and had moved on. We both were involved in other relationships, but legally we were still married. Months after I found out that my husband would also be expecting a baby by another woman.

I did not care what anybody thought. I had to hide this. I could not let anybody know. But no matter how good I was at keeping a secret, I failed to keep it from one person. That one person who would always remind me, always condemn me, and always tell me what a horrible person I was.

I was a murderer, a liar, and an uncaring and hateful person. I would never be able to escape this person's voice, and it would always be breathing down my neck. This person would always look at me with shame and disgust. I could not escape her, not even in my sleep. She followed me everywhere. I could never keep this secret from myself.

I was my worse judge, my worse prosecutor, and worst of all...I did not like myself. Now I disliked myself more than ever. It was bad enough that I had a child at a young age. On top of that I was an alcoholic, I smoked weed, I went to clubs, and let us not leave out the fact that I was sexually promiscuous. Oh no, those were not good enough reasons to despise myself! Now I was a murderer, a child murderer at that. How could I ever forgive myself? Would God really forgive me? If He did decide to forgive me, would He make me pay for my sins for the rest of my life? I lived with those tormenting questions and the torturing imaginations of what would become of me.

Ever since I was ten years old I was questioning God. I asked Him why I was so lonely and why my father would leave my mother and me to be with that woman. Why was my mom never there, and why was she not proud of me? Why couldn't I make her happy? Am I being punished? Did I mistreat people in a former life? Did I kill or lock people up in a prison so they would always be alone?

I had been tortured by the lies of the enemy since I was ten years old, but in the year 1998 I finally listened to that one voice that softly whispered in my ears, "I love you. I always have, and I always will."

In the spring of 1999 I surrendered my life to Him, and He began to change me, restore me, and give me back everything the devil had taken from me. Now I was taking back by force what the enemy had stolen. I was beginning to live in God's peace. The tormenting thoughts of not being worthy or loved would begin to slowly die because I found that I was created through His love. I was the exact representation of God's pure, unchanging, and unconditional love. However, I still allowed myself to live in the shame and guilt of my past.

Letting go and forgiving myself would be a very difficult process. What was actually easier for me was forgiving those who hurt me. I finally decided to forgive my mother, my father, Yanna, David, Jacob, Yovar, and anyone else who had hurt me. The root of bitterness was slowly being uprooted. But this root was deep.

I was trying to run from the sins of my past instead of confronting and dealing with them. Instead of allowing God to fully heal me and receive liberty from the shame and guilt of the things I had done, I tried to ignore and hide the sin. In a sense, I was trying to escape from myself. But how do you run away from your own shadow? Can you look in the mirror and not see your own reflection?

She was there everywhere I went. I thought she was my enemy. Her sins kept me in bondage. I felt as if I was chained to the shadow of my pain. This shadow was dark and cold. I believed it was so much greater than me. I could not run from her, so I allowed the nightmare of my past to devour me.

I continued believing the lies that I was nothing and that I would never be anything. I did not realize I was being deceived from the beginning. At the beginning my father hurt my mother, then she in turn hurt me, and then I in turn hurt Jerah. This virus was attaching itself to our minds and hearts. When my mother spoke to me through her hurt, the virus was released in the air, contaminating me with bitterness. The bitterness she felt toward my father affected me, then I became bitter.

I hated being bitter, but the hurt overtook me, and she represented hurt. Hurt caused from rejection, abandonment, and abuse. Because she believed in the lies of the enemy, she built a wall around her heart and held me a prisoner of my past. Although I had access to the keys to unlock the prison doors, I remained her prisoner because I felt safe behind the walls. I believed the walls would keep me safe from experiencing any more pain. If I unlocked the doors, I did not know what awaited me on the other side. I was afraid of the unknown; therefore I chose to live in the familiarity of dysfunction. I was her slave and she was my master. The only way I could be free from the shame and guilt was to face those demons. The only way I could confront those demons was to rely, trust, and believe in God to be my help.

Scene III

The Sting of a Bee

Do not rejoice over me, my enemy; when I fall, I will arise; when I sit in darkness, the Lord will be a light to me.

(Micah 7:8, NKJV)

Scene III: The Sting of the Bee

Angel: Why are you still here? He's waiting for you to get to the other side.

Destiny: I don't understand. Where is the other side?

Angel: Destiny, you are going around the same mountain again and again. You are in the wilderness. Do you not want to get to the Promise Land?

Destiny: I do not know how to get there. (Weeping now) I keep trying to follow this map, but it's getting me nowhere. I don't know what to do. I don't know how to do it! (On her knees frantically crying in a hopeless state).

Angel: For one, you are using the old map that many of your ancestors have used; therefore you are following their footsteps. The only way out of the wilderness is to pray and look to God, and He will direct your footsteps.

Destiny: Will you pray with me?

Angel: You do not need me to pray for you; you can always pray for yourself. However, I will pray with you this time.

Angel & Destiny: Father, destroy the generational curse and free Destiny (me) so that she (I) may reach the promise land.

Scene III: The Sting of the Bee

I could have entitled this: "A Date with My Daddy," "Seeking His Presence," "A Date With God," or "Save the Last Dance," but instead I chose "The Sting of a Bee." I made this choice because I learned a quick yet valuable lesson and, do not let me forget, a very painful one at that.

I took a couple of days off from work so I could get away to do some serious meditating and soul searching. I was going through some troubling things in my life. I was in a relationship that was not of God and having a difficult time letting go. My spirit was telling me to let go, but because I had left my heart unguarded, it began to deceive me. The one thing I was afraid of doing, I had done.

I tried to consume myself with the Word. I kept listening and studying God's Word. I would go into my "prayer" closet and get on my face asking God to give me the strength to let go. I even rededicated my life to God because I had backslid. I was getting all the knowledge and wisdom of God, but I had chosen not to walk in that wisdom. In addition to walking in His wisdom, I also needed to examine my heart. When I examined my heart, I found my motives were selfish.

I believe wisdom can be wasteful if you do not apply it. I also believe that God will tell us what we should do, but because we want things our way we choose not to obey Him. This relationship did not line up with the Word of God because I gave into the desires of my flesh to the point of losing control. The more I continued to remain in this relationship, the harder it was to get out it.

Keep and guard your heart with all vigilance and above all that you guard, for out of it flow the springs of life.
(Proverbs 4:23, AMP)

I wanted to make the relationship between God and myself right. And through this relationship my heart was revealed to me. To be honest with you, I did not like what I saw.

I decided to go to a Christian retreat. I would go there and walk along the water, just my Daddy and me. I really needed to get in His presence, and there is something about nature and especially the water that draws me nearer to Him. Maybe it's the wind that gently touches my body and combs through my hair. It's as if the Lord is caressing me and running His fingers through each strand of my curly hair. Perhaps it's the sound of the water slowly running up toward the shore. I heard His voice in every wave, and each wave carried the smell of marine life, which He had created.

I looked directly across the large body of water and to the right of where I stood. There were trees indicating wildlife was present. There were also a few homes where families may partake of this glorious beauty from sun up to sun down. Did they realize the gift they were given, or did they fail to appreciate a wonder right before their eyes?

I was going to savor every moment, every detail, every little boat, and every ferry that was anchored in the water. God gave vision and the skills to every person that crafted those vessels to carry people and cargo and yet float on water. Jesus was the only man I could remember who could walk on water. God in His goodness allowed us a small taste of the ability to be on water without sinking to the bottom as our lungs become filled with water.

I marveled at the pier and the man-made rock cliff with a light-house on the end. God was everywhere and in everything, even in the tiny drops of rain that fell on my body. Although this day was not filled with the brightness or warmth of the sun, it was still my day with God. Would a downpour ruin my recently shampooed and curly hair, forcing me to go indoors? Oh no, I came prepared with an umbrella in my gym bag! Nothing would keep me from hearing, smelling, or tasting the Lord. Besides, God knew that I loved the rain. It would make it all the more intimate.

As I sat on the bench overlooking the scenery, I was led to read Isaiah 50 (NIV). In verse 1, the Lord speaks to the people of Israel:

> *Where is your mother's certificate of divorce with which I sent her away? Or to which of my creditors did I sell you? Because of your sins you were sold; because of your transgressions your mother was sent away.*

In verse 2, the Lord continues to speak to Israel:

When I came, why was there no one? When I called, why was there no one to answer?

Stop right here! These two verses automatically spoke to my heart. "Because of your sins you were sold." I had allowed a married man to come into my life and into my children's life, but I didn't stop there. I gave my heart to this man.

Because of your transgressions [disobedience] your mother was sent away.

Now my mother was not literally sent away, but in my case for this particular situation I felt the Lord was telling me that since I had taken my heart from God and had given it away to a man, it was no longer in a safe place. Taking my heart from God caused a tearing or ripping in my heart. My heart was no longer under His protection or supervision as a mother would protect and watch over her children. Verse 2, again.

When I came, why was there no one? When I called, why was there no one to answer?

Since I had given my heart away, fallen to fornication, committed adultery, defiled my body and my home, my ears did not want to hear, or better choice of words, did not want to obey the Lord's voice.

I chose not to do what was right. I chose to do what made me feel good. I had turned my back on God and committed sin after sin. I was allowing myself to be conformed into who I used to be, a lover of the world, wanting to please my flesh while all along grieving the Spirit.

Do not be confirmed to this world (this age), [fashioned after and adapted to its external, superficial customs], but be transformed (changed) by the [entire] renewal of your mind [by its new ideals and its new attitude], so that you may prove [for yourselves] what is the good and acceptable and perfect will of God, even the thing which is good and acceptable and perfect [in His sight for you].

(Romans 12:2, AMP)

I was not as sensitive to conviction as I had once been. Let's continue with Isaiah 50:2-3 (NIV):

Was my arm too short to ransom you? Do I lack the strength to rescue you? By a mere rebuke I dry up the sea, I turn rivers into a desert; their fish rot for lack of water and die of thirst. I clothe the sky with darkness and make sackcloth its covering.

I looked at the waters and imagined the Red Sea parting in front of my eyes. I thought about the power of God. I looked toward the dark sky that had no trace of the sun in the sky that day. I read further, verses 7 and 8:

Because the Sovereign [supreme ruler] Lord helps me, I will not be disgraced. Therefore have I set my face like flint, and I know I will not be put to shame. He who vindicates me is near. Who then will bring charges against me? Let us face each other! Who is my accuser? Let him confront me!

I was concerned with the man I was dating in regards to his relationship with God. He was saved for years but had not dedicated his life to truly serve the Lord. I kept inviting him to church, but he would never make the time. He had other priorities, none of which placed God first. He had his own personal agenda, his own plans to make a happy life for himself.

Not only was I concerned with his walk with God, I was concerned with the way I was representing the Lord. None of us are perfect, but when you try to encourage other people to seek the Lord, it is very important that you are living a life that glorifies Him. You must put God first.

I was fornicating with this man! How could he really respect me as a woman of God? I felt ashamed of what I had done, and I was living in torment. I had allowed the enemy to deceive me for some time, and I was ready to confront him for the liar he was. I was ready

Scene III: The Sting of the Bee

to confront the old me and finally put her to rest. Truthfully, at times the enemy was myself. If we were completely honest with ourselves, we would admit that we are our worst enemies. However, God was near, and He was going to prove me innocent. We as children of God are not innocent by anything we do or do not do but by what Jesus has already done for us.

The blood would make me innocent, but I had to ask with a repentant heart for God to forgive me and cleanse me from my sin. When we sin we need to be quick to repent. Repenting is not saying, "Oops, I made a mistake, forgive me." No, it's turning away from that sin. We may not change the first time, but we have to be quick to repent, and the repenting should be in your heart. God's grace and mercy are not a license to sin. God will forgive you, but He will not take away the consequences.

> *Now I, the Sovereign Lord, am telling you Israelites that I will judge each of you by what he has done. Turn away [repent] from all the evil you are doing, and don't let your sin destroy you. Give up all the evil you have been doing, and get yourselves new minds and hearts. Why do you Israelites want to die? I do not want anyone to die, says the Sovereign Lord. Turn away from your sins and live.*
> (Ezekiel 18:30-32, my paraphrase)

The Lord is telling the Israelites to turn away from their sins or they will die, and He does not want them to die. He does not want you to die either. I am not speaking of a physical death but a spiritual death, however, I am not excluding the possibility of the first either. I know it is not easy. I am a living witness to that, but I can tell you the rewards for living in obedience are far greater than living in rebellion.

I did whatever I wanted whenever I wanted, but with each sin I was dying a little more. With every act and every word, my spirit was dead inside. But once I gave my life to God, my spirit was resurrected. I was reborn. I kept asking God for His forgiveness, but it was not in my heart to stop committing the sin. The more I sinned, the easier it became. It became easier for me because I had become insensitive to the conviction of the Holy Spirit.

I believe as Christians that we always want to blame the devil for the wrong that we do. But I think, in my case, it had little to do with the enemy and a lot to do with my own desires to please myself.

Instead of being so concerned with his walk with God, I should have been more concerned with my walk. The devil was not telling me to fornicate with this man; my flesh was. I wanted to do the things that were pleasing to the flesh, and I had no one to blame but myself.

Anyone remember the stand-up show Eddie Murphy did some years ago called Raw? Just to paraphrase, he said that when we get so hungry, even a saltine cracker will seem like a Ritz cracker to us. My body was hungry for a feeling of pleasure it had not felt in a very long time, and this man looked like a Ritz cracker to me. Now I am not trying to degrade him in any way, but he was not my husband. He was another woman's Boaz.

As I was reading from Isaiah, a bee flew by my face, and I quickly swatted it away with my hands. Now all who know me well know that I do not get along with bees! To be totally honest with you, I am terrified of them. I do not like them! While I was reading Isaiah chapter 50, verse 8, about the Lord being my vindicator, I felt this terrible, excruciating pain above my tailbone. I jumped up, dropped my Bible, and started to touch the area where I was attacked by that crazy bee. Well after a moment of performing an Indian ritual dance, I got myself together. I picked up my Bible and sat back down. Now afraid as I was of bees, why would I sit back down in the same place I just got stung? That is where the lesson comes in.

Now my back was throbbing from the pain of the sting. I could not seem to concentrate on reading anymore. Every little breeze made me think I was under attack by bees. My skin was tingling, my back throbbing, and I felt an eerie crawling on my chest. I looked down my shirt where I felt the creepy feeling, like a fingernail being dragged against a chalkboard. As I looked down my bra, I saw a bee slowly walking up the left side of my bra.

"Oh my God, oh my God," I kept saying in a silent scream as I frantically flipped my shirt open while jumping off the bench. I folded my shirt so the bee could peacefully fly out. "Get out, get out!" I

Scene III: The Sting of the Bee

pleaded with the bee. I could not smash the crazy thing or I would get stung again. I was at the mercy of the bee. I had to allow him to work its way out from my bra, and I could not force it.

All right, I had enough! It seemed like the bee had finally made its way out of my clothing, and I felt it was time to move on. I picked up my Bible and journal. I threw them in my bag and walked away from the bench toward the pier. That was enough fright night for the day.

As I left the bench where I had just experienced my lethal injection, passing the rock cliff with the lighthouse, I kept thinking about the pain. Although the sting did hurt, it did not hurt as much as I thought it would, or at least the way I acted any time a bee would fly close by.

I finally made it to the pier. I was not sure anyone was allowed to walk on it, so I looked at the sign posted at its entrance. I read the sign. The rules prohibited any sitting on the edges, along with a few other things. I read it all the way to the end to see whether or not walking on it was permitted. It was not prohibited, so I began walking down its wooden pathway, catching a glimpse of the wooden bench where I would soon make my resting place.

I was still a little shaken up by the bee sting. The throbbing started to intensify, and the experience of having that thing down my bra was excitement enough for me. I sat on the bench reluctantly massaging my sore back. I was afraid massaging would cause it to hurt more, but I could not help myself. I wanted the pain to quickly end. Regardless, I was not going to allow it to stop me from doing what I was there to do.

As I looked out into the water again, tears started to fall from my eyes. "I miss him, Father. This hurts so much (the fact that I had to end this relationship, not the bee sting, although it did hurt). I love him so much, God. How could I ever let go? Every time I tried to let go, I kept going back. Why do I keep allowing myself to be in a relationship that would hurt me? Why couldn't I have changed his heart? Why couldn't I convince him that putting You first in his life was all he needed to be happy? I tried to make him so happy, God, but I knew that I could not take Your place. I know that only You could complete him and fill him with a joy that no one or no circumstance could take away from him. Oh why, God?"

After asking a series of whys, I apologized for even asking. I knew deep down inside what the answer was. I told God that I would not ask any more whys but yield myself to hear His voice. However, I did say that I could not promise anything. I was into reasoning; therefore, I did not walk in peace, and I did not fully trust in God. He has always been faithful, but through this trial He was teaching me to TRUST in Him. How many times has the Lord been faithful to me? But through another test, I still wondered if He would come through. How many times did He rescue me on time, even though at times it was at the very last minute? But I still chose not to be patient. I chose not to be patient on the mate that He had already chosen for me. I prayed for a man who feared and loved the Lord more than he loved himself. I desired a man who respected God and hungered to get closer to Him. But again I was too impatient and decided to settle.

This was not the man that I prayed for. This was not the man that God had chosen to be the priest of my house, the leader of our home. I took my heart from God and gave it to a man who never truly loved me the way I should have been loved. The way God intended every man and woman to be loved. As a cherished treasure, more valuable than any diamond or jewel. To be desired more than a blind man longed to admire the bright smile of a mother he never saw. God intends us to be honored more than a loyal, noble, and righteous king of a nation. The love a mother, who was once barren, has for her newborn child.

In addition, what hurt more was the fact that I was not ready to be a wife. I was not in the place that I wanted to be for my husband. I had defiled my body and did not walk as the new creature God said I was when I gave my life to Him. I wanted to come before my husband as a spiritual virgin, made new by the blood of Jesus. The blood of Jesus had cleansed me from my sexual, immoral past, but because I did not receive it, I did not walk in it.

"Oh heavenly Father, I took my heart away from You, and now it hurts so much! I have to let go, but I am not strong enough. I need Your strength. Oh God, help me; please, please help me." As I continued to cry out to the Lord, He heard me, and His spirit spoke to me in the most soothing and comforting voice: "The joy of the Lord is your strength." At that point I just lifted my hands and sang to my God....

When I come into Your presence I humble myself
Lift up both my hands and I begin to worship You.
I worship You.
When I come into Your presence I humble myself
Remembering what You've done, The victory is won.
I worship You. I worship You.

My voice was shaky as the tears continued to fall down my cheeks and lips. My hands were lifted toward the sky, and I knew people were probably looking at me, but I did not care. I just wanted to praise Him. I just wanted Him to know how much I loved Him. I wanted Him to know that I was ready to give my heart back to Him. There was silence. I could no longer hear the water gently rushing toward the shore, only my broken and shaken voice as I sang psalms to Him. I knew that God was there. He was with me, wiping all my tears away.

For all You've done for me...
Redeemed and set me free...
Just because....
Just because
You're God.

Although I turned my back on Him and decided to do things my way, God still wanted my heart back. He stretched out His hands, and I placed my heart back where it belonged, back where it was safe. He had been waiting the whole time for me to give it back to Him so He could heal it once again. He would heal every wound and wipe away every tear. The Lord would mend my heart back together, as it was before I decided to walk from under the shadow of His almighty. No one was out there on the pier with me and I was facing the water, but the restaurant was right behind me and the windows were exposed for all to see. After I saw the bee fly away, for certain this time, I looked at the building to see if anyone had noticed the wild and crazy jig I just did. My hands were shaking and I was terrified by the possibility of there being more bees in my clothes. I could not get in the ladies room fast enough! As soon as I got in the rest room, which was completely packed with ladies who were there for a conference, I ran into one of the nearest available stalls.

I threw down my bag and started undressing. I was afraid that a bee would fly out of my clothing, but I did not care. I had to get my clothes off and off fast! After I stripped myself completely, socks and all, I shook every piece of clothing to make sure there were no more surprises awaiting me. After finding no evidence of any more black and yellow nectar and pollen-gathering insects, I thought about my hair. With all those curly locks there might be a chance that a bee could have gotten stuck inside! I started shaking my head and patting my hair with both my hands. After going through the punk rock dancing ritual five or six times, I did it one more time just to make sure. Then I looked into my gym bag to see if there were any signs of bees inside.

I slid the lock open and walked out of the stall, the stall that concealed a desperate search for one of my most feared enemies. I wonder what lady in the stall to the right of me was thinking as she witnessed clothing being dropped on the floor along with quick shuffling. I walked to the sink, thinking again, "Why is this happening to me? Why did that just happen?" My hands shook under the water as I tried to cleanse myself from the dirty feeling I felt from the incident that just occurred in the last half-hour. I walked up the incline that led to the lobby. Now my lower back and area below my navel were sore. The vision of the small hill with a bloody center that the bee's sting left entered my mind. It was a small sore, but the whole area below my belly button was aching. I could not see the sore on my lower back, but I could feel a large hill.

I looked out of the window at the pier I had just jigged the jig on, wanting so much to get back out there. The Lord was not finished speaking to me yet. As I opened the door, I told the enemy, "Devil, you are not going to stop me from coming out here." I started walking down the steps and immediately a wasp flew right in front of me. Okay, I thought to myself, this is warfare! I started pleading the blood of Jesus over my body, praying that no insect, spider, bee, or whatever would bother me anymore. I prayed for a hedge of protection

Scene III: The Sting of the Bee

from anything the enemy might have under his sleeves to keep me discouraged and in fear. I held my head up high with my sore stomach and lower back and started praising God once again.

Right then my spirit spoke to me, "So what did you just learn?" Oh my goodness, there was a lesson in those bee stings? Every time I got stung I kept asking God why, and now He was revealing it to me? My most feared enemy approached me on that bench, and I thought I had gotten rid of him by whooshing him away with my hand, only to find that he found a way to get closer to me.

The bee worked its way in my clothing and down my back. Once I got comfortable, thinking I had gotten rid of him since there was no trace of him anywhere in sight, I leaned back against the bench. It was then that I caused the bee to sting me. I was sore and a little shaken up because I did not see my enemy anywhere. As soon as I felt movement in my shirt, I found him there near my heart the whole time. I then jumped up, opening my shirt and thinking I had let the bee out so he could fly away. It looked like he flew away, but I really did not make sure that he was gone. At that point, I just started walking away frightened, sore, and disgusted.

When I sat down at the pier, I realized why there was so much pain in my heart. I worshiped the Lord, asking Him for His strength to help me let go when all the time I had the strength, but it was the selfishness in my heart that kept me from being obedient. I still wanted the relationship on my terms. Despite my rebellion, I continued worshiping Him and received a revelation. God still loved me although I was disobedient just because of the simple fact that He is God.

It was then that I had the uncanny feeling that something was in my pants. After I gently touched the area that the tickle was coming from, I again allowed myself to get stung by my enemy. The whole time he was there in my pants walking around. Just as the bee is my most feared enemy, another fear I have is being alone or being in a relationship with a man who does not love me the way that God wants me to be loved. I thought I had gotten to the point of ridding myself of the possibility that I would be hurt again from a man that I could love so much. I thought I had "swooshed" my enemy away, but there was something I was doing, something about me that attracted that enemy I did not want in my life.

I got comfortable by the false notion that I had "rid" myself (had been delivered) from getting into those unhealthy relationships again. I got comfortable thinking the bee was gone because I did not see it anymore. Similarly, I thought I was delivered from getting involved with an incomplete man who was led by his flesh. But you know if you are led to please your carnal desires, you will attract a person who has the same spirit. I had not been completely delivered from the spirit of fornication; therefore, I attracted a person who fornicates. I also had not been delivered from committing adultery and therefore had attracted a person who was willing to commit adultery.

Just think about it for a minute. You will see women or men who dress and speak a certain way. This person uses their body as bait, may hang out at the clubs on Saturday night, and then be on church Sunday morning praising the Lord. (Did I step on any toes?) They will end up being attracted to a person who does the same thing. Perhaps it is a person who does something that you once did; however, you still have desires to do those things. You will not see one of those brothers who go out to the club every Friday and Saturday trying to get with the sister singing in the choir, but wait, there are a few men who will try. Do you want to know why? Because there are Christian women out there who sing in the choir, who are involved in several ministries, but who are fornicating only to find themselves crying at the altar to be delivered.

I know what's up. Ladies, we have to stop fronting. I was one of those sisters while I was dealing with this brother. It does not mean that God loved me any less or that I did not love Him. It means I needed deliverance. Truthfully, we all need deliverance from something. However, God does say that if we love Him, then we will obey Him.

If you [really] love Me, you will keep (obey) My commands.
(John 14:15, AMP)

It means that I need to come naked before Him and repent (turn away from that behavior). I am not trying to glorify myself or justify what I have done. I just want to be real with you. I just want to let you know that you must get naked before Him. Tell Him your darkest secrets so He can bring a little light to your life. Why go on living in torment? I did for years. I found out what it felt like to have your heart in a safe place, and then you decide to take it from that shelter, only to have it broken again.

I was ashamed of calling myself a woman of God, knowing that I was turning my back on Him and asking Him to bless my mess. I continued to dig myself deeper and deeper into a pit, the pit of disobedience. I was with a man who really did not love me. He was a nice and generous person, but that is not enough. Women, the mate God has for you must have a heart for God. He must love God more than he loves his own life. He must be willing to protect your reputation, cleanse you with the Word, continually washing you and preparing you for God. He must present you to God one day. So ask yourself: Who have I chosen to represent me? Is he protecting my reputation? Is he a man who reverently fears the Lord and places God first in every single situation in his life? If you answered no to any of those questions, then please do yourself a favor and step back.

Where is your heart? Have you taken it from God? If you have, I could pretty much guarantee that you are not living in peace. You are torn and tormented by what the flesh wants and what the spirit wants. They are battling inside of you. God is waiting for you to surrender. Your heavenly and just God is waiting for you to become naked before him. Do not walk in shame anymore, because God is your vindicator. God will make you innocent before your enemies. Only He can do this, not you, and definitely not any mortal man.

Once I sat on the bench at the pier, disgusted that the enemy stung me, I got comfortable again. I thought I had rid myself from the one thing that caused and left me in pain. But the thought of him would not leave my mind. I kept missing him, wanting him back in my life, even though he hurt me. How many times do we women or men find ourselves getting back with the person who hurt us? Who we know is not the mate that God has for us? I hope I am not the only one. I got comfortable and thought I would be able to deal with the pain.

Now I'm busy praising the Lord while the enemy was still on me. He was walking around observing the territory, learning more about every part of me. The man I was dating was learning everything about me. He learned what did and did not make me happy. He found out just how far he could go. Because I chose to keep giving our relationship another try, I was letting him know that I would let him go pretty far. Men will do what women allow them to do. I let him know that I did not understand the value God has for me, so I was willing to compromise.

After I realized what was happening, he stung me again. So I had to get him off my skin, regroup, get naked, and step back out. Going forward, not back. I would not dare go back to that bench again. But was that the lesson in its entirety? No, once I realized I got stung a couple of times, I still had to move on with my life. I learned from my mistakes, but now I had to move forward and do what I had set out to do in the beginning. I had to get in the presence of the Lord and also fulfill the purpose He has on my life.

At the end of my visit at the Christian retreat, God saved the last dance for me. Another thing about me for those who do not know me well is this: I love the rain. You know at a date, there is always someone who asks you to save the last dance for them. God did not actually dance with me, but He provided a light shower as I stepped out from the place that taught me a lesson from a simple but very painful bee sting. My Father kissed me on my cheeks where tears once fell, took my hand, and walked with me to my car. "Thank You, Father, for being the best date I ever had. I love You so much, Daddy." I opened my umbrella and headed out toward my car as the sweet-smelling water fell from the sky while my feet stepped to a light beat.

Scene IV

Walking in My Destiny

Who has saved us and called us to a holy life—not because of anything we have done but because of his own purpose and grace. This grace was given us in Christ Jesus before the beginning of time.
(2 Timothy 1:9, NIV)

Scene IV: Walking in My Destiny

Angel: Destiny, where are you?

Destiny did not move in response to the call of her name. Did she not hear the angel call out to her?

Angel: Destiny (a little louder now), I am calling you. Why are you not answering me?

Destiny: Who me? I did not hear you call my name.

Angel: Well, is your name not Destiny? (The angel looked at her waiting for a response, but when she saw that she was not going to receive one anytime soon she continued with the task she was sent to do) God has a message for you, and He wanted me to give it to you with a sense of urgency.

Destiny: What is it? What would be so important that God would want you to tell me?

Angel: Destiny, God wanted me to tell you this: "Let go. Let go right now."

Destiny: What does He mean, "Let go"?

Angel: Let go of your past, let go of your fears, let go of Lorna.

Destiny: I thought I did let go of those things.

Angel: If you have let them go, then why do you not know that your name is Destiny? God says, "Let go now, or you will die."

BEGIN TO WALK IN DESTINY

As I am writing this book the Lord is continually preparing me for what lies ahead. I will never forget that statement, "To whom much is given, much is required."

But he who did not know and did things worthy of a beating shall be beaten with few [lashes]. For everyone to whom much is given, of him shall much be required; and of him to whom men entrust much, they will require and demand all the more.
(Luke 12:48, AMP)

We always want more, but we tend to forget the responsibilities that accompany the things we desire. I knew that revealing myself would result in enduring some things that I did not want to go through. I may lose the family I have, be left without any friends, and sometimes deal with being lonely, although the Lord would always be with me. May I be completely honest with you? Although I knew that the Lord would be there with me, I wanted someone I could feel. I wanted a friend available when I called to share my thoughts with. I wanted a husband I could physically lie beside, feeling his body next to mine. A husband that I could be naked and unashamed with and he not love me any less. A husband I would call my best friend.

I always struggled with being lonely, which was one of the reasons why I would continue ending up in unhealthy relationships. I figured he was better than nothing. Haven't we all heard that infamous saying, "Take it our leave it"? Who would have known that if we left it and trusted God that He would give us something or someone better than we would have ever imagined?

I would ask, "Why? Why has God chosen me?" There comes a price for every gift the Lord anoints us with. At times, it costs us our friends, and at other times it's our family. In some cases it is both.

Family members may warn you never to share your life with others. Your friends may discourage you and tell you what is "proper" or "improper," but I have to keep reminding myself of what God has called me to do and that I am a peculiar person. He reminded me that my life is a living testimony to be shared with others so that they may know what God can and will do in their lives.

> *But ye are a chosen generation, a royal priesthood, an holy nation, a peculiar people; that ye should shew forth the praises of him who hath called you out of darkness into his marvellous light.*
>
> (1 Peter 2:9, KJV)

One day I got on my face in my prayer closet and made a decision. "God, I give my life to You. Do not let my past experience be in vain. Everything the enemy tried to do in order to destroy me, turn it around and blow it up in his face!"

For the first time in my life, I honestly did not care what people would think of me. I did not care that I would be alone at times. I believed more than anything that everything I had was because of Him. In myself I was nothing, but in Him I was everything. I was made new. I was beautifully crafted by His hands, and I was acceptable by Him. He is the One that matters more than anything in my life.

Friends and family may judge you according to your past and not look at who you have become. They may think, while gossiping about you to their friends or other family members, "How could she say she loves God after all she has done?" Well, I am here to proclaim right now, it does not matter what I did in the past. What does matter is who God has made me today!

> *We know that our old (unrenewed) self was nailed to the cross with Him in order that [our] body [which is the instrument] of sin might be made ineffective and inactive for evil, that we might no longer be the slaves of sin. For when a man dies, he is freed (loosed, delivered) from [the power of] sin [among men].*
>
> (Romans 6:6, 7, AMP)

God the Father, God the Son, and God the Holy Ghost live in me and continue to change me every day from glory to glory. I must chose to submit to Him without complaining so that I may enjoy today and move on toward tomorrow.

Leave your baggage at the cross, and do not be like the Israelites complaining and murmuring making an eleven-day trip last forty years.

I found that I too was like the Israelites. I continued living in cycles due to all the fears I had. Walking in my destiny and fulfilling my purpose was the biggest fear of them all.

> *It is [only] eleven days' journey from Horeb by the way of Mount Seir to Kadesh-barnea [on Canaan's border; yet Israel took forty years to get beyond it].*
>
> (Deuteronomy 1:2, AMP)

FEARFULLY AND WONDERFULLY MADE

I found myself back to where I started, and I had to wonder why. Did I make any progress in my life? Why would I be back where I was two or three years ago? Have I not learned from the past yet? Have I not grown in the Lord enough that I would find myself back here again? This was my answer: I went back to a familiar place. Although unhealthy and painful, it was familiar to me.

My mind-set was stuck on getting used to the unhealthy and unfulfilled lifestyle that I had always been accustomed to. Instead of waiting for what God would have for me, which I knew deep down inside would be better than anything I could achieve on my own, I decided to settle. Settle for what I believed I deserved. Settle for what I allowed people to have me believe I deserved. I realized that I did not truly love myself. I did not truly know who God was, so I did not fully trust Him.

It was my second marriage; however, the marriage was not a marriage that glorified God. I believed, however, that the relationship was used so that I may see who God is in my life and for me to see how important I am to God. If truth be told, God is the only one who could give you what you need to the point that no one, no thing, and no situation can take that away from you.

God was revealing to me how I placed my husband, my situations, and myself above Him. I looked to my husband to be my only provider, my only protector, my only source of happiness, joy, and any type of fulfillment that I needed. Did I do it intentionally? No. But I did what was familiar to me, which was to fully rely on man and not God.

I also learned the hard way that being awesome at cooking, cleaning, caring for your children, and keeping yourself together physically does not keep a man. It is the heart of a woman who fears the Lord and carries herself with integrity, showing God that she loves Him by her obedience. It is the heart of a woman who knows that she is loved by God. She also knows that He only wants the best for her, so she must wait on the best that God has for her. Once she receives this revelation, she will begin to walk, talk, and show others that she will not stand for anything less than God's best. She can only get to that place when she gets to know who God is and who she is in Him. When she begins to know God and who He is, she will receive His love because He is love.

I finally believed the truth that God does not expect me to be perfect in order to bless me. God blesses me because He loves me and wants me to live a prosperous life. I believed that the only way to get anything good in my life was to do everything perfectly. I was a perfectionist, and I had placed my faith in my own abilities.

Each time my situation was not favorable, I blamed myself. I placed myself in a position where I was afraid to do or say anything that would place me in a position to fail. If my plans or relationships failed, I looked at myself as a failure. More often than not, I listened to people when they told me that I was the cause of the failures, especially those closest to me. Instead of them taking responsibility for their actions, they blamed me, and I would always accept the blame.

I realized that I am responsible for my actions only and not for the actions of others. Once I learned this, I began to walk in freedom from pleasing people. I found that I allowed myself to become a co-dependant of the responsibilities of others. Not only was I trying to buy the blessings of God through perfection, I was also trying to fix the shortcomings of others.

I was in the business of being a people pleaser. In addition to trying to buy the blessings of God, I was trying to buy the blessings of others. No one could ever buy blessings from God. God blesses us simply because He loves us. He is so much in the business of blessing that He also blesses those who do not even believe in Him.

Scene IV: Walking in My Destiny

...for He makes His sun rise on the wicked and on the good, and makes the rain fall upon the upright and the wrongdoers [alike].

(Matthew 5:45, AMP)

If someone truly loves you, they will bless you because of the love they have for you. Those who give to you only to get something in return only do so for their own personal gain. This behavior does not demonstrate the true love of God. I have heard many people, especially men, tell me they love me but never show me. Their definition of love was based on feelings, not what God defines true love as. Love is a choice, not a feeling. Love is sacrifice, not taking.

I was allowing others, due to their pride, to hold me accountable for their sins. Through one of the most difficult tests in my life, God had to remove those people, the ones I made my God. I placed everything I had in me into pleasing them instead of, not trying to please God, but making Him first in my life.

When you make people or things your god, you give that person, people, or thing power over you. I learned the hard way just how much power I had given people. Just as a drug addict or alcoholic goes through withdrawal when the chemicals are removed from their lives, I went through withdrawal. Even though these people were toxic to my spirit and soul, I still wanted nothing more than to be with them. My withdrawal lasted a few years, but I can now say I am free from people!

Most importantly, I have learned that I am the perfection of God. When He made me, He did so in His own image.

He was pleased and said that I am fearfully and wonderfully made. Thank You, Jesus!!!

I will praise thee; for I am fearfully and wonderfully made: marvellous are thy works; and that my soul knoweth right well.

(Psalm 139:14, KJV)

Testing My Faith

There comes a time in life when your faith is tested. You said, "I was your first love," but do you truly believe in what you say? My affliction, my trial, my test was to see if I really believed for myself that God truly loves me and if I trusted in what He said concerning me. No one could give me any answers. No one could advise me on what to do except God. Every situation and every person placed in my life from God all led me back to Him, and I was faced to look at the beginning, where it all began. So I began reading God's Word from the beginning. From the beginning God told His people that He would give them a land that flowed with milk and honey.

I read about several people who God had chosen to receive God's promise. These people had a lot of issues. The first issue that I saw was envy. Cain envied Abel because God was pleased with Abel's offerings to God. Instead of presenting God with his best offering, Cain murdered his brother. Jacob envied his brother Esau, so instead of thanking God for what God had for him, he tricked Esau out of his inheritance. Abraham and Sarah lied. Abraham lied to Pharaoh, telling him Sarah was sister instead of believing God would protect them. Sarah lied about laughing due to her lack of belief of having children at an old age instead of believing that nothing is too hard for God. I saw the spirit of deceit through Rebekah. Rebekah devised a plan to deceive Esau so Jacob would get the inheritance of the firstborn son.

There were liars, deceivers, murderers, etc. Nonetheless, God's promise for them never changed even when they lacked faith in Him. Moses questioned God about calling him to go to Pharaoh. Moses forgot God created him and knew what He asked him to do, and realized his situation regarding his speech. God calls us to do something not based on our qualifications or titles. Most often, God calls those who lack the qualifications in order to show that He is God. Therefore, the world would know that there has to be God, because without Him, achieving the task would not have been possible.

God was telling me that I needed to receive and have a full understanding of love. As part of understanding and receiving God's love, we must learn to love ourselves. I still had not gotten to the fullness of loving myself. I was always trying to please people and would always fail.

I found that we could never please people because we are not to be in the people-pleasing business if we are to be "on fire" and "sold out" for God. If you are truly serious about following God, you will show it.

I guarantee you will have enemies, and unfortunately, some may be the ones closest to you. Those who are really serious about you, who believe in you, and who will celebrate you are the ones you should stay in relationship with. Those who do not truly want God's best for you do not deserve to be in a relationship with you. That is a hard pill to swallow; I had to learn this one the hard way. But when I weighed it out, "God or man; man or God," there was no match. I went with God. I learned that I could still love them without having to remain in a relationship with them. I learned to let go and allow God to work the situation out. God will remove people who have no business being in your life if you are willing to let them go. Weigh it out: "God or man; man or God…" Go with God. I do not mean any harm, but He will replace those people with others who are "on fire, sold out" for the Lord, those who are lovers of God.

As I mentioned before, each time I failed at pleasing people, I believed that I was the failure, and most of the time those people wanted me to believe that I was as well. I would actually look at the unsuccessful results of pleasing people as a measure or reason to see myself unworthy.

In addition, I would give power to the negative things people would say to or about me. I would get upset with the lies that people spoke about me. I knew they were lies, but every time I heard the lies, I would get upset and would start defending myself. Every time I started reacting to the lie or those who spoke the lies, I was giving them and the lie power instead of believing that God's truth would prevail and that He sees all, knows all, and will deal with the lying tongue in His perfect will and His perfect timing. This took some time for me to finally "let go" and take back the power I had given to people and to the lie, but I did it and I was free.

It has been a long journey. I am just so grateful that God has been merciful in waiting, because He could, at any given time, have passed me by and given this assignment to another. There are many anointed writers out there that God has chosen who have created a new era in writing—T. D. Jakes, Paula White, Juanita Bynum, Joyce Meyers, just to name a few. They all have, through the power of the Holy Spirit, taken us to a new dimension. Needless to say, none of them could have written my story in the way that God has chosen me to do. So in saying all of that, I am again grateful for this journey that has been painful but necessary for the process and that has built character in me.

I am grateful for the call, and yes, I am grateful for the affliction because it is written, to whom much is given, much is required. My affliction has been painful, but it was well worth it because if I had not gone through it, I would still be the same pitiful lady walking, thinking, and talking in a victim's mentality. I am NOT a victim. I am a victor. I AM victorious in the Lord.

I finally received the answer I had waited so long to get. It was not as if God had not told me before, but I just was not in a place to receive it. You see, I was hindering myself from finishing a project that should have been completed years ago, but I knew if I did not have an answer for myself, then how could I help anyone else? Somewhere along the journey I got distracted. When I finally believed that Jesus is my first love, then God would bless me with my mate and he would be the result of the love I found in Jesus. I was wrong, dead wrong! What God wanted for me was to receive the love of Christ and then love myself. I had skipped loving myself and tried to give something away that I did not have. He also wanted me to dedicate my time in fulfilling my purpose and in Him, not in a mate.

I found that there are so many hurting people in the world claiming they love others but truly do not even love themselves. If they did, they would not behave in an abusive manner toward those they claim they love. That is not the love of Christ. Until we receive His love and love ourselves, the love we claim we have for others is some behavior that we "stuck" the word love on. The relationship you have with others is a reflection of the relationship you have with God.

You do not abuse people you love unless you are abusing yourself and your relationship with God. Do you truly love yourself, or do you cover up your insecurities by your outward appearance and worldly possessions? Do you truly love God, or do you care more about your relationship with man more than your relationship with Him? Are you a person who says one thing but does another? Are you faithful to others? If you are not, most likely you are not faithful to God. You may not be physically abusing someone, but instead you may be abusing them in an emotional or mental manner with your words and actions that usually stem from how you feel toward yourself.

I allowed things and people to distract me from staying on the road that would lead me to the promised land, and along the way my focus went from Jesus to people and the situations or circumstances in my life. I was so distracted that I fell into the act of idolatry. Whenever you put people, situations, or things before God, you have fallen into idolatry. We do this by thinking about people and things more than we think about the Lord. We consume ourselves with people, some of us our jobs or our worldly possessions. When we begin to consume our minds and thoughts on people and things more than we do God, we idolize them. When we idolize them, we magnify them and not God. I magnified what people said instead of magnifying what God said about me. I magnified the problems I faced more than I magnified the fact that God is the problem solver.

WHAT WOULD YOU GIVE UP FOR ME?

I was wandering around in the wilderness for seven years until I was in a place where I was faced with losing the things I cared about the most. God asked me a question, and I ran because I was afraid to answer Him, not knowing what would happen. But finally I could no longer run. I had to really search my heart, but my actions clearly revealed the answer that God did not want to hear. The question was this, "Are you willing to give up everything you have for Me?" I knew deep in my spirit that I really wanted to, but in my heart I was not willing. Without answering, because God already knew my answer, He replied, "Sometimes you have to give up that very thing you try so hard to hold on to and cherish in order to receive something greater, to receive what I have for you."

Now at the time I did not understand. I thought I had to physically give up the things I desired in order to receive something wonderful from God. But God was not going to stop blessing me if I decided not to let go of things. However, God wanted to bless me with all the wonderful things He desired for me. But I had to give up the things that I desired, those things that I placed above Him.

When God commanded Abraham to kill the son He promised him, Abraham by faith sacrificed his son in his heart. God made a promise to Abraham that did not change. God did not tell Abraham that if he did not sacrifice Isaac that He would go back on His promise. God is not an "Indian giver." He is faithful. Because of Abraham's faith in God, he was willing to do what God asked him. Just as Abraham made the decision in his heart that he would sacrifice Isaac, by faith I also had to give up everything in my heart.

Soon afterward I remembered hearing something said on a movie being shown on a Christian channel. The character who was portraying Jesus said, "Sometimes it takes great pain for us to finally realize how much we really need God." At that moment something happened in my spirit. I was being freed from the bondage I was in. At that very moment, while standing in my closet with tears running down my face, I shook my head in agreement and whispered, "I understand." I finally realized just how much God meant to me and how much I meant to Him. Not only did I realize I needed Him to help me through the pain, but I also realized that my very existence depended on having Him as the center of my life. Without God I would just be a mere memory to be forgotten like a leaf blowing in the wind. I understood that I needed God, because without Him I was truly nothing. I would not even exist if it had not been for Him. God meant more to me than all I was afraid of "letting" go.

THE QUEST FOR LOVE

Why are we driven to obtain love? Because God created us to seek after Him and He is love. We were made in His image to love Him first, to love ourselves second, and finally to love others like we love ourselves. He desires for our relationship with Him to be reconciled. Once it is, He desires for the awesome love that He fills us with to be shared with others.

Many of us have skipped over the vital step of loving ourselves. Many of us try to love others and spend our entire lives trying to please other people, only to find ourselves unsuccessful each and every time. Then we end up empty, dissatisfied, and disappointed in ourselves. We are always trying to figure out why by blaming the other person for the broken relationship due to our unsuccessful efforts. We fail to realize not only is it impossible to love others if you do not love yourself, but it is also difficult for the other person to receive your love if they do not love themselves as well. Instead of looking at ourselves and working on the areas that need change, we move from relationship to relationship. If we decide not to move to another relationship, we avoid them all together.

We must be accountable for our actions and repent. Repenting is not asking for forgiveness and then continuing to go right back to that sin. Do not use God's grace and mercy as a license to sin, because anything you sow you will reap. Your sin will catch up with you eventually. There are so many hurting people who refuse to be accountable for the things they are doing. They continue to live a life contrary to the Wword of God. They believe they can continue to say, "Sorry, forgive me, Lord," and then keep on with their actions. Read the Bible regarding sin. Sin not only affects you, but it also affects your family. If you are a parent and leave or neglect your children in some way, you can bet that your father and/or mother probably did it to you, and if you do not turn your life around, your son or daughter may do the same thing to their children.

RELYING ON GOD AND NOTHING ELSE

God has allowed me to experience the disappointment of people letting me down. The ones I relied on failed. The ones I depended on failed. The ones I trusted in failed. My own efforts, they failed. But I had to experience being disappointed with people. God did not want me to rely on, depend on, or trust in anyone except Him. I depended on finances from others, so He showed me that He is my provider. He provided for me every time I needed and with much more than I needed.

If you are the way I used to be, a perfectionist, trying to do everything perfectly, stop and be free right now. Every time you rely on people or yourself you will find yourself always disappointed. Nothing is wrong with bettering yourself and striving to grow in areas of your life; however, if you put so much energy and faith in your performance, abilities, and skills, you are relying on yourself more than you are relying on God. When you do not reach your standards, you end up disgusted, discouraged, and depressed because we depend on ourselves and not God.

We are blessed not by our college degrees or skills. Each morning we wake up is a gift from God. Every time we breathe air into our lungs, that is a gift. Every step we make is a gift. Every time we touch something and experience the ability to feel, that is a gift. God has also given us all awesome spiritual gifts, but we are so concerned with the gifts of others. Many of us focus so much on other people's gifts that we try so hard to be like them. But truth be told, those other people may be looking at and wanting what we have. We are not satisfied with our best because we believe our best just is not good enough. So what are we saying to God? "Lord, You gave me the wrong gift."

We all need change and growth. However, do not rely on your abilities and your own might to change yourself. Do the possible, and allow and believe that God will do the impossible. When you give up relying on people, including yourself, you will find freedom. People will continue to fail, and so will we. But the awesome thing about God is that He never fails and He will never give up on us. People will tell you that they will never leave you or give up on you, but many of them will when things do not turn out the way they like. They will go back on their word, but God will not. God will not be moved by your imperfections or failures. What He promises He will do, and one of His promises is that He will never leave you or forsake you. He also promises that nothing shall separate us from His love. I discovered that God is the one who I must fully rely on for everything.

When you try to share the promise and ministry God has given you with those you love, some may laugh in your face and tell you it will never work or discourage you in some other way. They may even disown you. But you have to go back to what God has said regarding you. We must stop giving people so much power over something they have not given us. Some of them may think they are helping us or giving us some good advice. Anything someone tells you should be a confirmation of what God has already said to you. People will judge you and tell you what they would do; just be very careful and pray about everything and do not do anything without going to God. He will give you peace about anything He tells you and the grace to get you through it. That person may be leading you into the wilderness, but God is trying to lead you to the promised land.

God had to ask me, "What did I say about your ministry?" Another thing about relying on yourself: God does not call the qualified, but He qualifies the called. Anything He has spoken in your heart to do, whatever your purpose in life is, God's grace is sufficient for you to accomplish it. As for your past, do not, do not, I said, do not allow what people say about your past or the way you may feel about your past determine your future. As Paula White says in Deal With It... God does not determine your future based on your past.

Know that your validation and worth should not come from others but only from the Lord. Do not base your value on what people think or say about you. Our worth comes from what God says we are in Him. We should not measure our value by our material possessions or our education. God never looks at our outward appearances or whether or not we earned a doctoral degree. God looks at our heart.

There are many wealthy and highly educated people who seem to have everything in their garages or homes that others dream of having, but on the inside of their souls they are empty and deal with rejection. We invest too much money on material gain, but we do not invest enough time on our heart issues. We are so quick to "show off" to the world what we possess. However, we hide behind worldly possessions and walk around with a phony smile. There are also those fake Christians yelling out their fake "Hallelujahs" and "Amens" after every sentence, while they are trying to cover up the hurt they carry inside. They are living lives that do everything except glorify God.

Fulfillment and completeness do not come from worldly value or relationships with man. Our completeness comes from the knowledge of who God is and what He says we are in Him. We can never enjoy the fullness of the life that God wants to give us if we do not know what He has promised us. How can we know what God has given us if we do not know who we are? We cannot receive our inheritance if we do not know we are related to that person. And how can we fulfill our purpose in life if we do not know what God has called us to do? Godly relationships are ones we all need; however, we cannot rely on people to give us what only God has the ability to give us. Only God can determine our worth and value. Only God can complete us. Only God can make us whole. Only He can give us total fulfillment, total joy, and total peace. Only God can give us provision to the point that we never lack. Only God can reveal to us our purpose and calling.

The Lord had to eliminate almost everything from my life in order to show me that He is my provider. Once you stop relying on people and yourself, you will find freedom from pleasing people and from being in a perfectionist mentality and life of self-pity. You will have freedom from those abusive people. You will have freedom to receive all that He has promised to give you. You will have freedom from people, self, circumstances, and situations. You will have freedom to live peacefully. You will have freedom to love, which is the freedom to receive His love, to love yourself unconditionally, and then to love others.

As women of God we have been created for a purpose. God saw it necessary to think and create us with complex systematic organs in our body, from the number of hairs on our head right down to the smallest birthmark we may have. God thought it not robbery to create us to breathe air into our lungs that would work to supply our cells with oxygenated air. We are not only women of God, but we are also daughters, mothers, and wives. Regardless of the hats we may wear, God has created and destined us for a special purpose that He wants us to fulfill. With that purpose, He has supplied us with the power through His Spirit to equip us for what He has called us to do. However, many of us have given our power away. We have given our power to people, situations, circumstances, our pasts, and the enemy. We have done this due to fear, insecurity, low self-esteem, self-pity, self-hate, rejection, and the list goes on. Let me tell you how we do this. I will explain to you this power that I'm speaking of that many of us have given away.

How do we give our power away? Let us first look at our relationships. Some of these points may seem to you as common sense, even so, we all do not use common sense but rather self-defense or self-survival. Instead of doing the things we know we should do, we take the route of self-gratification. When we do this, we ignore the consequences, thinking perhaps the pain was not that bad. You may not have gotten tired of it yet. Now you may be thinking to yourself, "I am definitely tired and sick and tired of being sick and tired." One way to prove it is to look around. If you are still in that same abusive relationship or in another one just like the one you left, then you are not tired yet. You have to be honest with yourself, which is something I had to do. There is truth in the statement: "The truth shall set you free."

And ye shall know the truth, and the truth shall make you free.
(John 8:32, KJV)

We spend so much time in our relationships trying to please people who never are satisfied with our efforts, because we are trying to do what only God can do.

Secondly, when we look at circumstances and situations and dwell on them so long, we have given them power over us. We consume our minds on those things and therefore have allowed those things to distract us from the things God has called us to do. Most importantly, we should look to God who is greater than any situation or circumstance. Only He could get us through it.

Thirdly, we have allowed our past to have control over our lives to the point where we are still in bondage of what happened yesterday or even years ago that we cannot change or fix. We have given our power to our past or better yet to the grave, and we do not even enjoy our life now and we dread our future. I myself have allowed people to use my past against me. I have allowed people to judge me, label me, and condemn me because of my past, which was already covered by the blood of Jesus.

Lastly, we have given the enemy power over us. How do we do that? We sometimes give the enemy too much credit. If you find yourself speaking of the devil more than God, you have given Satan power. "The devil made me do it" is entirely overrated. Do you not know that we are our own worst enemy? We do things because we choose to go against the Lord. It is not always the enemy. Stop using him as a scapegoat for your willingness to sin against God. Stop giving him so much credit, and begin speaking more about the power of God and His faithfulness, His goodness, and the power and the authority God has given us to trample on our enemy!

The only solution to this madness is God. We cannot please people; only God can, but even then some choose to reject Him. If people seem to be unsatisfied with you and you have done all you can to be the child of God, know that their void can only be filled by God. There is nothing left for you to do except to continue living a life that glorifies God. And if you find yourself proving or defending yourself for being something God had already confirmed about you, or if you are trying to prove your innocence to a rumor being said about you and lies be spoken against you, know this…God is your vindicator, your advocate, and your judge, and above all else, His truth will prevail.

God is our advocate:

My little children, these things write I unto you, that ye sin not. And if any man sin, we have an advocate with the Father, Jesus Christ the righteous.

(1 John 2:1, KJV)

You have been giving power to that person or people and to those rumors and lies. God will, in His time and in His way, reveal the truth. It is so difficult to stand, be still, and not say anything because you want so badly to defend yourself of a crime you know you have not committed. But when you are still, you will begin to see God move. Just pray for that person or those people and rest in His peace. Just remember and be comforted to know that Jesus also experienced rumors and lies. Jesus was also rejected by His own people whom He loved and came to die for.

BETTER NOT BITTER

I am no longer bitter but better. I realized that I had given power to the pain, but I learned that only Jesus has the power to take the sting out of the pain. Jesus is the healer of the brokenhearted:

> *He heals the brokenhearted and binds up their wounds [curing their pains and their sorrows].*
> (Psalm 147:3, AMP)

We as people cannot heal the hearts of another, and if your gift is in healing, it is not you who holds the power but the Holy Spirit who has given you that gift.

> *Now there are diversities of gifts, but the same Spirit.... To another faith by the same Spirit; to another the gifts of healing by the same Spirit.*
> (1 Corinthians 12:4, 9, KJV)

As children of God (I pray that you have already given your life to God), we can no longer operate in the spirit of manipulation or control in order to get someone to love or treat us a certain way. We must give up our attempts and give that person to God. Our energy should not go into trying to change anyone. God will touch the heart of those who have hurt you. The energy you spend is like throwing a coin into a wishing well. Situations, circumstances, and the heart of a man cannot be moved or changed by wishes. We must release and relinquish our will to God. Fully trust, fully rely, then fully rest and believe in Him.

We must have faith that God will do all He needs in order to change you. Yes, I said, "in order to change you." God will change you so that you can stand and weather any storm that comes your way. He will not always change the circumstances, the situations, or the people that we may face. However, God will do such an awesome work in you so that you may stand in whatever adversity comes your way in the attempt to steal your joy. So in the spirit you will look at the situations, circumstances, and the people in a different manner. If we continue to ask God to change everything that is uncomfortable in our lives, and God were to do that, then we will never grow spiritually. When Jesus died and was resurrected, the Holy Spirit came to comfort, teach, counsel, and to do whatever needs to be done in order for us to stand and walk in the purpose God has destined for us.

> *But the Comforter, which is the Holy Ghost, whom the Father will send in my name, he shall teach you all things and bring all things to your remembrance, whatsoever I have said unto you.*
>
> (John 14:26, KJV)

God says He has given us grace that is sufficient. Therefore, if you are going through something now, it is because God has allowed it and He knows you can make it through by His Spirit and His power, not by your own might. We must believe that He is able and will do all that we ask. Therefore, ask God to prepare you for the process and high calling He has specifically for your life. There will always be uncomfortable situations and circumstances, as well as people, that we will confront in our lives. But God has provided us with the equipment and armor we need to stand in every situation.

Whatever you go through, do not allow it to leave you bitter. Learn the lesson from it so that when you come out on the other side, you will be better. When God changes you, you will no longer look at your circumstances as stumbling blocks, but instead you will see them as stepping-stones. You will begin to step on each stone and find yourself at a higher level than you were when you first began your walk with God.

When you first give your life to God, the enemy will be angry because you are now a threat to him. He will begin to throw stones at you. The first stone may be this: "You ain't saved. You think that little prayer saved your life and that you are going to heaven?" Then, "Look at you, you are still messing up! Why would God forgive you?" He will also throw this stone: "You ain't no good! Your mamma (or your daddy) told you that you would grow up to be nothing, and she (he) was right!" Then, "God does not love you." With each stone he throws your way, seek God and not man or your own intellect for your answers; believe what God tells you. You will start walking on each stone and see yourself become more mature in the spirit. Let me help you with those stones that I just gave you as examples.

Stone 1: "You ain't saved. You think that little prayer saved your life and that you are going to heaven..." The devil's lie.

God's truth:

And they said, Believe on the Lord Jesus Christ, and thou shalt be saved, and thy house.
(Acts 16:31, KJV)

And he said unto me, My grace is sufficient for thee: for my strength is made perfect in weakness. Most gladly therefore will I rather glory in my infirmities, that the power of Christ may rest upon me.
(2 Corinthians 12:9, KJV)

Stone 2: "You ain't no good. Your mamma or your daddy said you would grow up to be nothing..." The devil's lie.

God's truth:

Since all have sinned and are falling short of the honor and glory which God bestows and receives. [All] are justified and made upright and in right standing with God, freely and gratuitously by His grace (His unmerited favor and mercy), through the redemption which is [provided] in Christ Jesus.
(Romans 3:23, 24, AMP)

Therefore if any person is [ingrafted] in Christ (the Messiah) he is a new creation (a new creature altogether); the old [previous moral and spiritual condition] has passed away. Behold, the fresh and new has come!
(2 Corinthians 5:17, AMP)

Stone 3: "God doesn't love you." The devil's ultimate lie.

God's truth:

For God so loved the world, that he gave his only begotten Son, that whosoever believeth in him should not perish, but have everlasting life.
(John 3:16, KJV)

Who shall separate us from the love of Christ? Shall tribulation, or distress, or persecution, or famine, or nakedness, or peril, or sword?

(Romans 8:35, KJV)

For I am persuaded, that neither death, nor life, nor angels, nor principalities, nor powers, nor things present, nor things to come, nor height, nor depth, nor any other creature, shall be able to separate us from the love of God, which is in Christ Jesus our Lord.

(Romans 8:38, 39, KJV)

And walk in love, as Christ also hath loved us, and hath given himself for us an offering and a sacrifice to God for a sweet-smelling savour.

(Ephesians 5:2, KJV)

In this is love: not that we loved God, but that He loved us and sent His son to be the propitiation (the atoning sacrifice) for our sins.

(1 John 4:10, AMP)

And from Jesus Christ the faithful and trustworthy Witness, the Firstborn of the dead [first to be brought back to life] and the Prince (Ruler) of the kings of the earth. To Him Who ever loves us and has once [for all] loosed and freed us from our sins by His own blood.

(Revelation 1:5, AMP)

Every time a stone or stumbling block comes your way, stand on God's Word. As God renews your mind with His truth, the stumbling blocks will turn into stepping-stones.

If it is poverty:

I have been young, and now am old; yet have I not seen the righteous forsaken, nor his seed begging bread.

(Psalm 37:25, KJV)

The thief comes only in order to steal and kill and destroy. I came that they may have and enjoy life, and have it in abundance (to the full, till it overflows).
(John 10:10, AMP)

Above all else, as you step up onto each stone to a greater level in the Lord, remember these two very important things:

1. **God never lies.**
2. **The enemy always lies.**

God is not a man, that He should tell or act a lie, neither the son of man, that He should feel repentance or compunction [for what He has promised]. Has He said and shall He not do it? Or has He spoken and shall He not make it good?
(Numbers 23:19, AMP)

Accordingly God also, in His desire to show more convincingly and beyond doubt to those who were to inherit the promise the unchangeableness of His purpose and plan, intervened (mediated) with an oath. That was so that, by two unchangeable things [His promise and His oath] in which it is impossible for God ever to prove false or deceive us, we who have fled [to Him] for refuge might have mighty indwelling strength and strong encouragement to grasp and hold fast the hope appointed for us and set before [us].
(Hebrews 6:17, 18, AMP)

You are of your father, the devil, and it is your will to practice the lusts and gratify the desires [which are characteristic] of your father. He was a murderer from the beginning and does not stand in the truth, because there is no truth in him. When he speaks a falsehood, he speaks what is natural to him, for he is a liar [himself] and the father of lies and of all that is false.
(John 8:44, AMP)

The enemy will always lie to you about what God has already promised you. What the enemy meant for your harm, God will use for your good. Choose to become better and not bitter.

Forgiveness Is a Choice, Not a Feeling

I have learned the difference between forgiving and forgetting. With forgiveness you release the person from the hurt they have caused you. You pardon the sin, and in return you receive freedom from the sin and place the situation in God's hand. God will heal your heart, take the sting out of the pain, and work in that person's heart. God says not to take revenge for ourselves. He will repay. As long as you keep unforgiveness in your heart, you are trying to make that person pay for what was done and you remain in bondage.

Forgiveness does not mean forgetting what was done or said to you. You will remember the action, but through the process of forgiveness, God will take the pain associated with that action away.

Forgives does not mean we accept the behavior. I have learned the difference between meekness and weakness. Walking in meekness means we are humble and we think of others higher than we think of ourselves. It does not mean you idolize them and degrade yourself. It means you love them and want the best for them without selfish motives. This is true ministry, something we are to operate in every day of our lives. With meekness you do not accept behavior that would harm you physically, emotionally, mentally, or spiritually. We are to stand firm in our faith but speak the truth in love.

I have learned the difference between true love and an imitation. I have found that true love is a choice made that is demonstrated through sacrifice. The one who loves another sacrifices himself for the other without compromising who he or she is. The one who loves another is patient, believing the best of the other person. The one who loves does not keep a record of the wrongs the other person has done; however, he does not accept the act to continue on. Love forgives, but it does not justify, defend, or take responsibility for the action or for what was said. I learned that Jesus represents all these things.

He sacrificed His life for me but still remained who He was and stood on His precepts and statues. Jesus loved me even when I did not love myself. Jesus does not remind me of the wrong I had done but allowed me to learn through the consequences of each sin I committed. Therefore the consequences made me a better person, and God worked everything out for my good. Jesus forgave me and continues to forgive me. However, He does not tolerate sin. God hates sin, but He loves the sinner. I found true love in Him. Jesus has taught me that true love begins with Him, but it never ends. Through receiving His love for me, I have learned to love myself. His love was the answer to all my questions. His love allowed me to forgive even though I will never forget.

Closing

Closing

These past eight years have been difficult, but I have been truly blessed. Since I began this journey, I have wandered in the wilderness for quite sometime. I went through this continuous cycle of trying to find out who I was while still relying on people, the past, and my circumstances to dictate to me my value and worth as well as my identity. Being a Christian does not mean we will fly on cloud nine the moment we say, "Lord, forgive me. I surrender my life to You." Nor will we see a miraculous sign, lightning bolts, or any other natural occurrence. Well, at least I didn't.

I believe Christianity means I have been reconnected to that relationship, a relationship once severed by sin, and promise that I will no longer have to lack any good thing with God. Throughout this Christian walk, we will endure persecution, violence, rejection, and abandonment, but we will not lack anything. How can we still endure all of that and still not lack any good thing? I found that because God loves me, when I endure persecution, He will lift me up. When I endure pain, He will comfort and heal me without leaving any scars. When I am rejected, He has already accepted me. And when those I love abandon me, He has adopted me. God is truly my all in all, and if I had to do it all over again, just to be able to know Him the way that I do now, then it would be more than worth it.

Throughout this book, I continued to refer to myself as Lorna (remember this means lost, forlorn, forsaken), because that is what I believed I was. Understand God had called me something else before He even formed the foundations of the world. God called you something before He formed the foundations of the world.

If you believe you are a nothing, worthless, helpless, a victim, etc., then you have not tapped into what He says. I am trying to get you to understand something. Truth remains the truth whether we believe it or not. I could tell you the earth was flat and if you went too far you would fall off, but the truth is the earth is round. I do not believe it is round. I believe it is flat, but does that change the truth that the earth is in fact round? Recall our history when some men believed the earth was flat. It is what they believed, but it did not change the truth. According to God, we are wonderfully made; that is truth. He says we are called, He says He loves you, He says all you have to do is confess your sins and believe in your heart and you are saved…see, the word is believe. You must believe.

I did not believe the truth, but the truth did not change despite my beliefs; however, my actions dictated what I believed in. So I walked around lost, forlorn, and forsaken, and my actions showed it. What do you believe regarding who God calls you and what He has promised you? Have you given your life to Him? What are you waiting for? Tomorrow is not promised. Confess your sins and believe in your heart that Jesus is the Son of God who died on the cross for your sins.

Be free.
Free from your past.
Free from what the world says about you.
Free from anything that would hinder you from receiving the fullness of life that Jesus died on the cross for you to have.
Be free to receive God's love for you.
And
Be free to love yourself.

Closing

SINNER'S PRAYER

God, have mercy on me.

I humbly come before You as a sinner asking You to forgive me for every sin I have committed.

I believe in You and that Your Word is true.

I believe in my heart that Jesus is the Son of the living God.

I believe in my heart that Jesus died on the cross, was resurrected by God, and is living now.

I believe in my heart that Jesus' blood was shed for my sins that I may have eternal life with Him.

I give my life to You and ask You to take full control.

I pray this in the name of Jesus Christ.

Amen.

HALLELUJAH!!! The angels in heaven are rejoicing.

THE BEGINNING

But seek ye first the kingdom of God, and his righteousness; and all these things shall be added unto you.
(Matthew 6:33, KJV)

Closing

RESOURCES FOR VICTIMS OF ABUSE

If you find yourself in an abusive relationship and do not know where to turn, understand that there is help for you. If you have lost hope, hold on because help is on the way. During my last marriage, due to the abuse, my children and I stayed in a shelter for six weeks. It was a lot longer than I would have ever anticipated, six weeks longer. I want to share with you some of the resources that are available for abused women. I can only share what I am aware of but I am sure there should be more. Look in the phone book or on the internet for help.

RESOURCES:

If in Delaware:

Delaware Victims of Crime: 1-800-VICTIMS1

They will direct you to the appropriate persons for your particular need.

Domestic Violence Hotline: 302-762-6110

Delaware Legal Volunteer Services (DVLS): 302-478-8680

DVLS will assist you with an attorney for Protection From Abuse (PFA) orders. They may be able to get you an attorney free of charge.

Delaware Family Court: 302-255-0300

To file the following orders: Protection From Abuse Order (PFA), Child Support, Child Visitation, and Child Custody. They also have a Victim Advocacy department inside the Family Court building that will assist you in the PFA process.

Victim Advocacy: 302-255-0420

Delaware's Domestic Violence program continues to provide services even after you are out of the relationship.

Nationwide: Domestic Violence Hotline 1-800-799-7233

Website: www.ndvh.org

About the Author:

I was born at the Thai Naval hospital in Sattahip, Thailand in 1973. According to the Thai Calendar that would be the year 2516 BE (Buddhist Era). Just add 543 if you were born after January 1, 1941. Why haven't I given you the month and day? Well, let me explain in what I call, "The Controversy Regarding My Birthday."

Just recently, I informed my dad that I had been celebrating my birthday on February 5th for the past few years now. For as long as I could remember, he always celebrated my birthday on February 1st. I explained to him how I came about this date. In my explanation, I told him about the conversation my mom and I had concerning my true birth date. She explained to me that she had gone into labor this particular Sunday at the beginning of February, and I was born the following day. She further stated, "If you want to know your birth date, look in the 1973 February calendar. Check the first Monday in February; that's the day you were born."

Guess why she had me do the work? Because I don't believe she honestly knew the date either! She did, however, know it was not the first, second or third of February - the three dates I had heard in my childhood years. When I explained all this to my dad, he broke it down in more detail.

He explained that he had gone on the road on a Sunday night, which placed him in Bangkok, Thailand, on the Monday morning. He told me that my mom had complained of having pain that Sunday. He was on the road several days and returned that Thursday. There is a Thursday in 1973- February 1st. When he had returned to find my mom doing laundry in the backyard, I had already been born a few days earlier. Props to my mom! She is my Super-Mom/SuperWoman, truly deserving of an "S" on her chest.

I told my dad that he might have gotten the 1st of February from the date he actually returned home and had been welcomed by the news, "Dino (his nickname), you have a baby girl!" Given the scenario of the days and the events and my dad having the 1st in his mind, then I would have been born in January. Things that make you go…"Hmmmm."

Since my father was not there, a friend (Naval soldier) of my parents took my mom to the naval hospital in Sattahip, Thailand. Their friend only knew my parents as Dino and Wandee, so those were the names placed on my birth certificate. My mom went back to Sattahip to get their names corrected on the birth certificate and was informed that the names could not be changed at that location. Instead, she was directed to go to Uttardit, her birth place in Thailand, to make the changes. Since my mom was ill, my grandmother went to make the corrections. That was on August 26, 1973. She was given the option to keep the date I was actually born, versus the date she arrived at the location. The difference in cost was $5.00 for the actual date of birth, versus $2.50 for the August 26th application date. Guess what my grandmother chose as a date? You guessed it! August 26, 1973, my legal birth date.

When my father looked at the birth certificate, it was written in Thai since we were in Thailand! My dad finally got it translated, but at that point it was a legal document and nothing could be done.

A few years later, my parents and I moved to the United States and eventually were stationed in Fort Riley, Kansas. By the time I was around five-years-old, my parents were divorced. Shortly afterwards, I no longer spoke my native language, Thai, but instead, moved from being taught more Thai to teaching my mother how to speak, read and write English. I did have the wonderful opportunity of watching my mother take night classes to learn English more on her own, and later on, to receive her United States citizenship.

Growing up in a single parent family and being the only child was very lonely. Sadly, my best friend was my dog Tiny, who lived to be 133-years-old (dog years).

When I was about twelve-years-old, my mother remarried. My stepfather was very abusive verbally, emotionally, and physically towards my mother. I remember times when I ran through the house screaming and crying, when he would be on top of her beating her. It was not until one particular night when I decided I could not take it any more.

"Stop hitting my mommy!" I shouted. That night, I defended my mom and my stepfather did more than cuss me out that night, he struck me. What is funny about the entire situation (if there really is any humor in it) is that he went to the police station to press charges against me. When the police officer telephoned the house, he asked me how old I was. After I answered him, he asked me why I had hit my stepfather. I told the police officer it was "because he was hitting my mom." The officer said, "Good for you." That was the last time I heard about my stepfather trying to press charges against me.

In August of 1986, my mother had her second child, my brother. Soon after my brother was born, my mother divorced my stepfather. About a year later, I had my first child at the age of fifteen. Eric was born in Newark, Delaware, where I lived with my paternal aunt. I lived with her a few months and then stayed with the daughter of my son's babysitter, and her family.

For the first time in my life I finally understood what it meant to live in a stable family environment with both parents. I truly enjoyed living with them. They enrolled me into Del-Castle Vocational High school where I wanted to take nursing courses; however, plans changed. They decided that they needed to give me and my mother an opportunity to build a relationship together. Despite my begging and reasoning with them, they did not change their minds. Once Eric was about nine-months-old, we were on the plane back to Junction City, Kansas.

The relationship between my mother and I was torn, due to the fact that I now was a teenage mother. The thought of that was painful and difficult for my mother. Up to that point, my ultimate goal in my life was to make my mom proud of me. I truly wanted to make her happy. Once I found that I couldn't possibly do that, I gave up. We argued constantly, and I found myself living with a friend, then Eric's father and mother, and for the first time, at the age of seventeen, alone with a new boyfriend, when I experienced Domestic Violence firsthand.

It took me several months, a bloody nose, and a black eye to finally open my "good" eye and get out of that relationship. That experience truly humbled me. I no longer judged my friend, whom I continued to question, "Why don't you leave your boyfriend? You're too smart and pretty to have someone beating on you?"

I was married at the young age of nineteen, shortly after that (six months) I was separated, and then after six years, divorced. After graduating from Kansas State University with a Bachelor's Degree in Science, and now pregnant with my daughter, Asia, I (along with my son and my boyfriend) moved to Delaware. I wanted to build a relationship with my father and hoped to obtain a career in my field. As with the other relationships, my daughter's father and I broke off the relationship. In addition to being abusive to me, I found him to be abusive to her as well.

After a life of several unhealthy relationships, I thought I finally married the love of my life after our first daughter, Samara, was six-weeks-old. Unfortunately, I found myself in another abusive relationship. After several months of emotional, mental, and some physical abusive, and then finally being verbally threatened that he would kill me, we finally separated. During our separation, I strongly hoped and prayed that our marriage would change. After several attempts to reconcile, I found myself again pregnant. This time with twins - Alexia and Alexandria. My lifetime desire to have twins was now being filled, but our marriage was damaged. Still hoping that God would perform a miracle, despite seeing my husband drink, party, and have relationships with several other women, I submitted my will to God.

"God, I surrender to You my desires and accept Your will in my life." Eight days after the twins were born, my husband filed for divorce.

In spite of all that happened in that marriage, I have been so blessed. During the separation of my ex-husband, God promised me that He would redeem everything I had lost, everything that was stolen, and everything that I gave up, and has given me better than I would ever imagine. He promised me that He would redeem my tears of sorrow with tears of joy. He also promised that He would redeem the TIME! What kind of God is that who would redeem time? I can truly say He has redeemed all that, and He has just begun!

I have never had so much joy and peace in my life. I am now single, but I am truly loving it! I have been blessed with so much more than I could ever imagine. I thank God for choosing me for such a purpose as this, and I pray that you would come to know Him personally. I pray that you would be changed and delivered by the testimony of my life.

Like I said…"This is just the beginning!"

Be Blessed,
Be Renewed,
Be Free,
And receive all that God has in store for you…I am.

www.ingramcontent.com/pod-product-compliance
Lightning Source LLC
Chambersburg PA
CBHW070452100426
42743CB00010B/1581